Find Freedom Fast:

Short-Term Therapy That Works

Say Goodbye to Anxiety, Phobias, PTSD, and Insomnia

Robert T. London, MD

Kettlehole Publishing, LLC
New York City, New York

DISCLAIMER

To protect the privacy of certain individuals whom the author describes herein, their names, physical characteristics, and other identifying details have been changed as well as the creation of composites of symptom groups and people so as to protect privacy.

This book is designed to provide general educational information about the subjects discussed and not to diagnose, treat, cure, or prevent any physical, psychological, or emotional condition. It is not intended as a substitute for any diagnosis or treatment recommended by the reader's psychiatrist, psychologist or any other medical practitioner. Use of this book does not establish any doctor-patient relationship between the reader and the author or publisher.

The author has made every effort to ensure the accuracy of the information within this book was correct at the time of publication. The author does not assume and hereby disclaims any liability to any party for any loss, damage, or disruption caused by errors or omissions, whether such errors or omissions result from accident, negligence, or any other cause. No warranties or guarantees are expressed or implied by their choice of content for this volume, and there is no guarantee that these materials are suitable for the reader's particular purpose or situation. If you suspect you have a physical, psychological, or emotional problem, we urge you to seek help from the appropriate specialist. This book is not intended to be a substitute for the medical advice of a licensed physician or mental health provider.

Neither the publisher nor the author shall be liable for any physical, psychological, emotional, financial, or commercial damages, including, but not limited to, special, incidental, consequential, or other damages resulting from the use of this book. Please be aware that references to other sources are provided for informational purposes only and do not constitute an endorsement of those sources. The methods described within this book are the author's personal thoughts. They are not intended to be a definitive set of instructions. The reader may discover there are other methods and materials to accomplish the same result.

Dedication

This book is dedicated to my original family, who was there for me from the beginning—my father, Dr. William London, a leading eye surgeon, and my mother, May London, the most understanding and supportive mother a person could have. And to my current family—all the Londons, big and small: Joyce London, Esq.; my two sons, Michael London, Esq., the plaintiff's lawyer standing up for the many; and Daniel London, an internationally recognized pharmaceutical advertising executive; and their respective wives Sarah Shine London and Heather Combs London, Esq., two women who have genuinely enriched the entire family with their intelligence and kindness, and who besides their own accomplishments together have brought six lovely grandchildren into the world (Darby, Jack, Avery, Charley, Chloe, and Theodore). To my sister, Ruth, and niece, Shari, as well Uncle Jack London, whom we call Great, Great Jack, and his wife, Aunt Charlotte (who makes the best Thanksgiving dinner on the planet).

And to the Shine and Snow-Reddington families, and especially Denis and Carolyn; and to the Combs family in Kentucky, Ralph, Gail, and Todd.

This book is for you.

Acknowledgments

A very, very special thanks to my book editor Jana Martin, for her skill, creativity, and guidance.

Special thanks as well to Gina L. Henderson, my newspaper editor at Clinical Psychiatry News. Over two decades, I developed and published columns on Learning, Philosophizing, and Action, as well as on issues about interface of psychiatry and medicine. I've always loved great twentieth century American writers like Ernest Hemingway, F. Scott Fitzgerald, and Thomas Wolfe. Their editor at Scribner's was the great Max Perkins. I'd say Gina is my own Max Perkins.

Another very special thanks to the memory of my lifelong friend, Donald Bain, who started his writing career with the great book *Coffee, Tea or Me?* developed the scripts for my radio show, and encouraged me over and over to write a book until finally, I did.

A great thanks to Dr. Elishka Caneva, a gifted psychiatrist who believes in short-term treatment strategies. She reviewed some of my ideas on short-term therapy techniques and offered invaluable suggestions on the current state of psychiatric training and care.

A very special thanks to Dr. Jonathan Brodie, who was kind enough to write the foreword. I first met Jon when he was a third-year psychiatric resident in the short-therapy program I was running at NYU Medical Center. Little did I know the great genius within him, including his far-reaching contribution to medical advances while completing his PhD, his successful professorship at NYU Medical Center, stepping in as the interim chairman of psychiatry when the need arose, as well as a skilled psychiatric clinician for those many patients he has treated.

To Cliff Barrett and Frank Gorin: I broadcast from their syndicated radio company, BGI, offering sound medical advice to thousands of Americans. Cliff and Frank insisted on taking me to lunch every second Monday when I recorded my shows.

To Dr. Herbert Spiegel, the psychiatrist and teacher who started me on a career of short-term treatment strategies, and Dr. Herbert Walker, whose supervision in behavior modification techniques enriched my education. To Dr. William Frosch, my residency director, who gave me the key to an office in the old Bellevue Hospital outpatient clinic and let me begin my short-term psychotherapy program with smoking cessation and weight control. To Dr. Leslie Forman, who joined me in this short-term unit and offered great insights in Cognitive Behavior Therapy.

Additional thanks and dedications are in order—for this book would not have been possible without all of the doctors, other professionals, and friends I've come to know in my life, or those who taught me when I was a student and resident. To the memory of Dr. John K. Robinson, the dean of students at University of Miami, Miller School of Medicine, whose door was always open to offer support, guidance, and wisdom when I was a medical student there. Dr. Robinson was always supportive and ever present at those wonderful alumni parties we developed and held with his associate dean, Barbara Binns, whose door was equally open for guidance and suggestions. To dean Dr. Bernard Fogel, U. of M. Miller School of Medicine, whose guidance was always appreciated. Trained as a pediatrician, he provided great insights during my rotation in his specialty. A special thanks to Dr. Burt Goldberg, my family doctor, who for many years called himself a "chicken soup" doctor. But his constant availability and knowledge rated him as world-class to the thousands he served. Thanks as well to his lovely family: his wife, Doris Goldberg, and their children: Dr. Doug Goldberg, Dr. Gary Goldberg, and Susan Goldberg, R.N., Ed.M., M.A. May this book honor the memory of Burt and Doris.

To my good friend Dr. Leslie Goldberg, his lovely wife Zehava, and their children Shelley and Michael. Leslie was the eye surgeon who stepped in and took over my father's medical practice, developing it into one of the finest eye surgery facilities on Long Island and who also loves cars. To Gary Douglas, Esq., my son Michael's law partner, who brings the best focused common-sense answers to the law anyone could ever want, and to his lovely wife, Pilar Douglas, Esq. To the memories of Dr. William Schick and Dr. Walter Kass, two of the greatest supervisors during my training at NYU/Bellevue. To my many wonderful and supportive friends over the years, including Dr. Ed Weiss, the best internist/cardiologist in the world, and text-messenger responder, as well as his lovely wife, Ellen and of course, Iris Aviles, who makes things work, Dr. Susan Polizzi, who, besides her vast medical knowledge, actually makes time to speak on the phone.

Thanks to Dr. Donald Marks, the best dentist in the world. To my friend, Dr. Alfred Culliford, the great cardiac surgeon—who besides his lifesaving work, endlessly supports advances in mental health, as well as Dr. Sripal Bangalore for his kindness and support plus Dr Richard Lebowitz for his friendship and great otolaryngolical skills. And to the great friendships that I treasure with Joe and Sue Bruck, Linda Strong Friedman and her family, Dr. Harvey Barash (the best and smartest person in the world to work with) and his lovely wife, Martha. To Dr. Fazil Hussain, a true encyclopedia of medicine, and his family. To Dr. Richard Overfield, who always reminds me to teach more often. To Dr. LaVonna Branker, a very smart internist, Dr. Marissa Kaminsky, who knows how to use the psychiatric medications with great success, Dr. Howard Liu, a fine ophthalmologist friend whom I talk cars with, Maria Leventis, N.P.; Anna Golden, N.P.; and her husband, Tom; to Dr. Beatrice Spinelli, to Joyce "Tobe" Rocamora-Geller, my oldest friend, as well as Richard Girasole, CPA and Ed Rich, retired CPA, who are always there with great answers, plus Ron Ramirez, Esq. and Lynn Sculley, Esq., who provide great insights and information, as well as, Denise Gibbon, Esq. a great contract specialist and of course Daniela Diaz-Arbelaez for her thoughtful, diligent and technical assistance. To the friends of my sons who as adults became my friends: Dr. Michele Pauporte; Stacey Lowenthal; Josh Fagin; Sam Lewinter; Steven Kay, Esq.; Craig Bruck; Zack Weiner; Dave Balderson; Dave Morgan; Jarred Isaacs, and their respective wives and partners. To Dr. Michelle Crimins, Dr. Larisa Gaitour, Nicole Breck, LCSW psychiatric social worker, as well as Robin Allen Kaynor, MSW. And a special thanks to those lovely people and friends at the old Beatrice Inn in Greenwich Village, where my whole family enjoyed great food and spent so much time in the 1970s and 1980s, and my newer friends at Chelsea Ristorante—where you get a warm reception and wonderful food. All of these had a hand, direct or not, in my inspiration to write this book, and I hope you know how much you are valued.

Table of Contents

Foreword

When I first met Bob London over 40 years ago, I was a senior resident in psychiatry at Bellevue Hospital with an academic career in biochemistry. Bob was a young, quixotic, and creative assistant professor of psychiatry who espoused views of psychiatric treatment that I had never before heard a supervisor espouse.

Focus on achieving symptom relief, he told us. Assume that the primary role of the treating physician is to first address the patient's chief complaint, and then work from there in terms of reducing the patient's stress.

It might be hard to believe now, but Bob's approach was novel, refreshing, and somewhat heretical at the time. Still, he won me over. I have told patients from the time I began practicing psychiatry that my job was to become unemployed.

The course Bob taught was entitled "Strategic Psychotherapy." It taught us hypnotic strategies that would help the patient develop behavior awareness and decision-making skills until he could ultimately control conscious and unconscious behaviors such as smoking and overeating. He was ahead of his time in identifying the importance of behavioral techniques to address self-defeating behaviors. As Bob demonstrates in this book and its examples, the therapist should use the patient's strengths to minimize his weaknesses and the patient's cognitive resources to mitigate the helplessness and lack of control that lead to maladaptive lifestyles and self-defeating behaviors.

The hallmark of Bob's style and the success of his targeted therapy rest less on textbooks and theory, and more on the powerful interaction of the psychotherapist and his patient. This leads to a sense of patient empowerment and mastery, or as Bob puts it, "awareness," that many behaviors are indeed approachable, improvable, and can be controlled by the patient as the result of conscious choice. He contended then and continues to contend that many people want to have an issue fixed, and not enter a lifelong or multiyear contract to understand "the why." When he began his targeted approach to psychiatric presentations, he was an outlier. Now, he is much more mainstream.

What Bob realized, way ahead of his time, was that the patient's strengths, combined with the therapist's experience and training, could enable the therapist to devise a strategy that would address the patient's most immediate needs. Rather than being formulaic, neutral, and dispassionate in regard to the patient, Bob emphasized each patient's uniqueness, i.e., presentation, abilities, personality, and skills. He realized that these attributes could be used by an astute therapist to achieve a mutually desired therapeutic result. In other words, Bob contended there is no reason for the therapist to hide behind regressive psychoanalytic techniques or "one-size-fits-all" behavioral paradigms as an excuse to not address the issues that first caused the patient to seek therapeutic help.

Rather than requiring the therapist to suppress his own personality, Bob urges a team approach that uses the skill sets of both parties—engaging the therapist's knowledge, intelligence, caring, and experience while employing and re-enforcing the patient's capacity for self-empowerment and responsibility. This approach not only engages the patient and encourages the patient to use his own skill sets but also emphasizes that the role of the therapist is to help the patient address these issues. The anecdotes in the book, presented as case histories, help the reader appreciate just how unique Bob's approach was and is. I am honored to be one of the generation of students who benefited from the universality of the principles he developed.

In this book, Bob says to both patients and fellow therapists: Your personality is part of your toolbox—do not be afraid to be who you are, but embrace your assets and strengths to minimize weaknesses. Do not sacrifice the "what" while striving for the "why," and focus, focus, and focus on addressing the principal complaint.

This is Bob London. You can feel his personality and his passion. This is his book. The philosophy and case histories are distilled from his experiences over many years of writing, thinking, and teaching. Countless articles, lectures, and editorials have not dulled his passion. Enjoy!

Jonathan D. Brodie, PhD, MD
The Inaugural Marvin Stern Professor of Psychiatry, Professor Emeritus of Psychiatry New York University School of Medicine

Introduction

Life is short, this we know. The dance from birth onward goes very fast. We all dream about things we want to accomplish: Act in a play, write a novel, get married, lose weight, finally let ourselves take that vacation, or just enjoy a rewarding life that's well-organized and stress free. But among the many roadblocks that stand in our way, none is as profound as time itself. Day after day, people don't do what they wish they could. "Forget about time," a patient once told me. "What I don't have is the courage to move on the way I want. I simply don't believe I can do it."

Well, I don't agree. We all have the power to make changes as our life moves forward, and what better time to begin than right now? This is your life, not a dress rehearsal.

The Time Is Now

I'm a psychiatrist who believes in helping people take charge of their own lives. Over many years of practice, I've developed a method of short-term psychotherapy called LPA (Learning, Philosophizing, and Action). It's a unique and effective combination of Cognitive Behavior Therapy (CBT) approaches that can help you end troubling behaviors, control your fears and anxiety, conquer a phobia, and free you of nagging doubts or poor self-esteem. Added are the techniques of relaxation, guided imagery, hypnosis, and a variety of tried and true behavioral, and cognitive behavioral modification strategies that can be learned quickly and used for a lifetime as part of this LPA method.

As I look back on all the people I've worked with over the decades, I want to guide or help even more so that many of you don't need to spend years in a therapist's office just to free yourself of a problem that's been holding you back and accomplish your goals. So why wait? If there's a way to find freedom fast by fixing an issue—why not begin some of those things right now?

For many years, I've been writing newspaper columns—and receive a lot of positive feedback from psychiatrists, psychologists, and other mental health professionals. I also hear from regular people, all across the country, who want to know more about my LPA method and how it can help them with problems they face every day. Their questions and stories are what prompted me to bring my ideas and experience together in this book. My goal is to show how many commonly experienced problems can be resolved in a short time span—by focusing on learning new ideas, concepts, and behaviors, and by keeping the focus on fixing the problem at hand. You *can* find freedom fast.

The traditional approach to therapy is a long journey. Session by session by session by session, the patient talks, and the therapist offers his or her theoretical interpretations, serving as a sounding board. Hopefully, the patient's realizations will gradually begin to unfold.

That process can take months, often years. The decision to see a therapist may well be initiated by a specific problem, but the therapy won't necessarily focus on it—in fact, it may lead you down a completely different path (also known as the "we'll get back to that" methodology). Traditional therapy may turn into an extended, unlimited once-a-week exploration of the patient's entire life and set of experiences. It's not unlike the old psychoanalytic method, which mandated four or five sessions a week, but now many of those same ideas are packed into once-a-week visits, each full of open-ended, theoretical, non-problem-oriented talk. So it's a long commitment: it's got a beginning, and as many people have reminded me, it's got a very long middle, because, depending on the therapist, it may not really have an end. Sometimes it reminds me of the 1973 movie *Sleeper*, in which Woody Allen wakes up from a very long nap and says, "I haven't seen my analyst in two hundred years. He was a strict Freudian. If I'd been going all this time, I'd probably almost be cured by now."

A Surgical Approach

My LPA (Learning, Philosophy, and Action) technique is different. As I often say to my patients, let's think about what we're doing here. What's the goal? LPA targets one specific problem, maybe two. Working together, we find out how best to resolve it by circumscribing the problem, challenging it, and acting to change it. That's the goal: solve the problem so you can leave it behind and move on with your life.

Sounds practical, right? There's a very good reason for that. I grew up in a medical family. My father and uncle were both surgeons, and they were practical men. Their profession demanded it. When a patient checks into the emergency room with an eye injury or a ruptured appendix, a surgeon assesses the problem and takes immediate action to fix it.

Let's say you've broken your leg on the ski slope. The attending physician might ask a few relevant questions about previous injuries, allergies to pain medications or anesthesia, but if she suggested you start your treatment by discussing your history as a skier, whether you took an unnecessary risk by venturing onto that black diamond trail, how your parents felt about risk-taking, and how that affected your childhood, you'd think she was wasting your time. Your leg is broken. It hurts. And you want the doctor to fix it, fast.

When people come to me in distress with a psychological problem that needs to be solved, I take the same practical approach. Identify the problem, ask the necessary questions to start moving forward, and get to work. Fix the problem. Move on from the distress. Open up to new ideas and perspectives. Once we've accomplished that, you may choose to delve further into the ongoing issues that fed into the problem, that's fine, but you won't be walking around on a broken leg while you do it.

My father was an eye surgeon. His specialty was helping his patients to see better. I like to think I do the same thing, but where he focused on the physical mechanism of seeing—the eye itself—I help my patients to see the specific issues better and solve the problems before them.

A Surgeon's Son: How I Started

My surgeon father was not overwhelmed by my choice of psychiatry as my medical specialty. Nevertheless, he was very supportive and even started subscribing to psychiatric journals. And though he may not have realized this, my choice may have been inspired by his own approach as a doctor. On many occasions when dealing with difficult patients, my father would say that their problems were "in their heads," whether it was headaches with no physical cause or a set of glasses that fit perfectly but the person simply didn't want to wear or acknowledge needing glasses.

I vividly remember one patient who called him at home all the time, an anxiety-ridden man with recurrent headaches and anxiety but no physical illness, who must have been an undiagnosed PTSD patient from WWII based on what I heard my father saying. My father endlessly reassured this patient that he'd be okay and tried to get him to adjust his thinking in many different ways during the many telephone conversations I overheard. Could it be that my father unwittingly planted the seed of my interest in Cognitive Behavior Therapy (CBT) before it even came of age?

I can't help but wonder how much overhearing these interactions with suffering patients influenced me to become a "head doctor." My father felt strongly that psychiatry did not do a lot to solve people's problems. He said it either made patients sick with medications or hospitalized them for too-long periods of time (ironically, now hospitalizations are often too short), which removed them from the community where they needed to function, or trapped them in endless sessions of treatment that got them to hate their mothers.

When I declared my interest in psychiatry, he tried to guide me into focused short-term treatments. His fatherly wisdom for me was, "If you're going to be a psychiatrist, learn something most of others in the field don't know." I felt exactly the same way and thought it was great advice. There had to be a better way to help people who suffered from many types of emotional problems than loading them with medications or stringing them along with some sort of therapy that focuses on unsubstantiated unconscious longings and getting angry at your parents.

During my residency at NYU School of Medicine/Bellevue, I was surprised and dismayed that most of the program was devoted to psychopharmacology and psychoanalytic/psychodynamic therapy that focused endlessly on symbols from one's unconscious and past family patterning, usually blaming somebody else for your problems.

My interest was in more focused short-term treatments based on learning theory, not unlike the way we all learn in school. And of course, growing up in a surgical family, it was natural to want to circumscribe the problem and solve it as quickly as possible.

I attended a number of short-term treatment seminars that were good, but focused on traditional psychoanalytic concepts that were shortened and a bit more interactive. I was not really satisfied with this approach, as the patient examples all seemed to need continuing care afterward, i.e. long-term therapy.

One of my teachers in the residency program was Dr. Herbert Walker, an expert in behavior modification who allowed me to spend extra time in his seminars and actually see how short-term therapy based on relearning concepts could work.

In my last year of training, I attended a life-changing course at New York-Presbyterian/Columbia University Medical Center, directed by Dr. Herbert Spiegel. The course focused on medical hypnosis and behavior modification, and with the great skills of Dr. Spiegel, CBT was integrated into his wonderful seminar. He was clear in demonstrating and teaching treatment strategies for habit and pain control, including smoking cessation and weight control. He also applied these techniques to the treatment of anxiety disorders, phobias, and what would emerge as a broader definition of PTSD (post-traumatic stress disorder) in the 1980s.

After this Columbia University seminar that changed my thinking and direction in psychiatry, I asked Dr. Spiegel if I could continue to study with him. He was as gracious as ever, and set up a weekly seminar program for two colleagues and me that went on for a year. What a great learning experience from a master clinician and a legend in short- term psychotherapy techniques!

The following year, I joined Dr. Spiegel's annual seminar program at Columbia University Medical Center. Over the next five years, I became a more and more active participant in teaching, really fine-tuning my skills in short-term therapy. Dr. Spiegel was as masterful a teacher as he was a clinician.

Next, I set up my short-term therapy program at NYU School of Medicine/Bellevue, where I taught hundreds of residents in psychiatry over a twenty-year period. I also developed my CME (continuing medical education) program at my home base, NYU/Bellevue, as well as bringing these seminars to my medical school at the University of Miami, Miller School of Medicine.

More than thirty years ago, I began writing professionally for newspapers and magazines offering informative columns on a variety of clinical and social issues that can be helped by getting a better perspective and understanding using short-term therapy techniques. And I developed my own form of CBT, which I call LPA (Learning, Philosophizing, and Action).

Launching the LPA Method

My therapeutic method is as practical as they come. Over a very short time span, I guide the patient through three steps—Learning, Philosophizing, and Action—that lead to a simple, everyday under-standing of how to fix many emotional problems. LPA's origins were goal-based right from the start. This wasn't a method I created to en-able my patients to contemplate their navels. They didn't have time for a Freud-inspired "talking cure." They had an immediate problem to solve.

When I began developing this approach decades ago, it was part of a special program I created within the New York University Medi-cal Center. After learning and practicing smoking cessation with Dr. Spiegel at Columbia, I had the idea to bring this technique over to NYU Med and start using it to help many of Bellevue Hospital's patients, along with some Bellevue and NYU staff members, to stop smoking. I asked my residency director, Dr. William Frosch, if I could begin a short-term therapy program based on behavior modification, starting out with a smoking cessation program. Dr. Frosch was fine with this. Even though he was a classically trained psychoanalyst, as a dedicated educator, he was able to see a bigger picture. So began the short-term psychotherapy program that I would run for twenty years.

The program was designed with a targeted therapeutic focus. Though I later expanded it into a short-term therapy program with multiple facets, originally it was dedicated to trying to help patients accomplish a very specific goal: to stop smoking. The only thing they wanted my help with was giving up cigarettes.

We're complicated beings, and it can be really, really hard to quit a deep-rooted habit like smoking. But as we all know—and as my pa-tients knew—smoking can kill you. So on a very pragmatic level the point was to save lives, as effectively and efficiently as possible. The habit of smoking was interfering with people's lives, and causing myr-iad illnesses and premature deaths.

Had we embarked on a long-term therapeutic relationship, where every week I sat down with a patient for 45 minutes and explored this or that, the patient could have developed lung cancer, emphysema, cardiac disease, or other illnesses as we delved into the possible meanings of that one dream from the age of nine, or an oral fixation, before we even started to focus on smoking. And another thing: if I were going to truly respect my patients' wishes, what had brought them to me was their wish to stop smoking. That wish became my mantra as I laid out the groundwork for a three-point, goal-oriented, self-help program of smoking cessation over the very short term but with the aim of lasting a lifetime for our newly non-smoking patients. The program was very successful, not only in smoking cessation, but as a lead-in to weight control strategies as well as a diversified short-term therapy program. It helped me develop and fine-tune the LPA techniques I still use today.

The smoking cessation program was a one or two visit self-help program based on comparing or juxtaposing the value of one's life with the smoking habit/nicotine addiction. It was my modification of the program pioneered by my great mentor, Dr. Herbert Spiegel, using hypnosis and behavior modification techniques to link the patient's goal in stopping a disastrous habit/addiction with the value of life, and it included teaching this self-help model so patients could continue to use these techniques long after they finished the one or two treatment sessions.

Narrow Focus, Broad-Based Changes

People are not used to thinking about therapy as a specific, isolated, short-term process of focusing on specific problem, but that's exactly what LPA is. I didn't need to delve into my patients' childhoods for months, or lead them into an illuminating but endless foray on why they don't feel satisfied with their jobs or relationships. We didn't ignore those causes or ignore the behavior that developed from it, but we got through it faster, because the point was to take action. Remember, I needed to get my patients to stop smoking, fast.

And here's what happened: The more focused we were, the better we were able to solve the problem. I also noticed that my patients actually took comfort in knowing this process had a beginning, a middle, and an end. It made them braver. The structure gave them the confidence that they could accomplish their goal. They just had to follow the steps, practice the techniques, and they'd get there. The short-term framework, with its three specific phases, gave them courage.

This book includes many examples of people overcoming a wide variety of issues. You'll meet otherwise healthy people with phobias they've been unable to shake, people with general and situation-based anxiety, and people who responded to traumatic events in their past or present with symptoms of PTSD. These case studies offer a magic road, showing how each and every person can Learn, Philosophize, and Act to gain new perspectives and move toward change for the better. This includes *you*.

The most important concept I want every reader to understand: If you want to make lasting change in your life, the key is to get a new perspective on the old set of problems. Change is the most elusive part of talk therapy, and your eventual success will be linked to finding a new way to look at the problem that has been holding you back. With that change of perspective in place, you can see things differently and start *doing* things differently, yielding a better result.

Sometimes I ask patients, "Where do want to be next month, or next year, or in five years, or ten years?" The answers to these questions, along with the step-by-step, practical techniques of LPA, will help you start making the changes you want to achieve.

An unsolved problem stands in the way of your happiness. It's messing up your life. The goal of LPA is to fix that problem so you can find freedom fast. But here's the silver lining: the result, I've found, is far larger than the solution itself. Once the problem is solved, my patients are happier, and they can move on with their lives. We don't try to fix their whole life. We just tackle the problem at hand. But because we are people with souls and spirits and psyches, because we're not one-dimensional, and because everything has an effect on everything else, solving that one problem can have enormous results. Solving that one problem can help resolve problems in other areas as you learn and use these techniques as new issues arise in your life. These kinds of results make this short-term, three-part therapy as profound and life-changing as it gets.

Now, let's get to work.

CHAPTER 1

Trapped in Therapy: The Problem with Psychiatry and Psychotherapy

Cognitive Behavior Therapy and short-term methods such as LPA have been extremely effective at treating a wide variety of problems. So why do so many therapists start with a long term approach with people spending so much time in these therapies that can drag on almost forever. Why not start short-term specific CBT problem solving methods first, then go to longer term care if need be and the person would like to explore more.

Well change moves slowly in the mental health community. Part of this has to do with the way psychiatrists are trained: Many therapists with a variety of degrees (and some without degrees) still use the methods that were current when they trained—or more accurately, when the person who trained them trained. Other methods go back even further when fewer options existed.

Training for Treatment

Psychiatric training takes a long time. So does training to become a clinical psychologist; they are PhD's. Psychiatric social workers train beyond their master's degrees, as do psychiatric nurse practitioners, who first must become registered nurses. In the twentieth century, a myriad of therapies and therapeutic techniques were developed that offer a wide variety of approaches. However, psychiatrists are MD's. We're required to complete a college pre-med program and a four-year medical school degree before we can focus fully on our field of specialty. To become a psychiatrist, we must complete four *more* years of training in a psychiatric residency. Much like a surgical residency or pediatric residency, this is the hands-on part of our education.

Let me break it down. For psychiatric residents, the first two years are spent in inpatient work, working in hospital settings where we rotate through different areas of care (adult, child, adolescent, and geriatric) along with seminars, reading assignments and presentations, as well as emergency room training and psychiatric consultation in other medical specialties, including medicine, surgery, and pediatrics. The final two years are spent in outpatient work, educational seminars, and supervision on the current patients whom the psychiatrists in training are treating.

The outpatient work is divided into segments, which may include different treatments:

- Psychopharmacology
- Psychoanalytic
- Interpersonal
- CBT (Cognitive Behavior Therapy) and DBT (Dialectical Behavioral Therapy)
- Psychodynamic
- Supportive
- Group
- Family

Getting Past the Past

The inpatient work is pretty clear, usually focused on medications that are appropriate for severe depression, bipolar disorder, and thinking disorders (generally grouped under the umbrella of the schizophrenias, with hallucinations and delusions as dominant features) as well as educational and supportive care. But in outpatient care, a great deal of training still adheres to outmoded concepts of how our brains work. These outdated concepts may have been groundbreaking in Freud's Vienna, but that was the nineteenth century. Hasn't our understanding of the brain and behavior evolved since then? Yes, Freud did bring one-to-one medical care and an office setting to mental health care, abandoning terrible treatment practices, and his followers added to this legacy. But some of their ideas—still used in treatment today—are at best fantasies of these intelligent people's imaginations.

I'm going to take a dip into my own past in order to shine a light on psychiatry's rear-view mirror. As a child, I suffered from countless sore throats and ear infections, and was treated by a neighborhood doctor as well as my father, who was a doctor and a surgeon. When I was about five years old, my father offered to drive me to school one day. He had never done this before—and some part of my child's brain must have wondered why he would drive me to school when we lived right across the street from it. But I'd always loved riding in cars with my dad, so I agreed.

I was excited as I jumped into the back seat of his steel-gray Buick sedan. He pulled out of the driveway and drove down the block as I stood in my favorite position, on the floor right behind him, leaning against the back of the driver's seat so I could watch him steer. (This was in pre-seatbelt days.) I remember on long trips to my visit uncle and aunt in New Jersey, I would stand in this position for the whole trip, even falling asleep on my feet.

At the corner of our block, we made a right turn onto the main local avenue and drove at least twenty blocks away from the school. When I asked where we were going, my father told me he had to make a stop first. Suddenly he pulled up and parked right in front of a big hospital. Because my father was a surgeon, I'd had the experience of waiting in the car while he made a post-op call to see one of his patients, something that was done much more often back in those days. But this time, he told me to come with him. Of course I did, but I began to feel anxious immediately as I trotted along, trying to keep up with his long stride.

We went through the main entrance of the hospital. My heart was already starting to pound when a scary-looking nurse with gray hair grabbed me by both arms, lifting me right off the ground. My father said sternly, "Take it easy," but she already had me in her grip and whisked me away.

The next thing I remember, I was put in what looked like a cold white bedroom, where someone in white clothes took blood from my arm. Of course I was terrified. Why was this happening? Where was my father, and why had he brought me here? What would my mother say when she found out?

I remembered that she hadn't given me any breakfast that morning. Now, of course, I know why, but at the time it just added to my feeling that nothing was normal that day. They put me onto a hospital gurney, like a tall bed on rattling wheels, and I was whisked down a long hall to an operating room. The same gray-haired nurse with the mean face was there. As she leaned over me, terror took over. She put a mask over my mouth, and I started seeing all sorts of colors.

The next thing I knew, I was in a bed. Someone was giving me ice water to drink. As I recall, I was quite calm. My father and mother were both in the room. My father told me that my tonsils and adenoids, which had been causing so many sore throats and earaches, had just been removed. I would not be sick anymore, he said. I must admit I was quite happy. My father told me that a doctor our whole family knew—an ear, nose, and throat specialist—had been the one to operate. He also told me that he himself had been in the operating room the whole time, and told me that I had been brave. I would be going home soon, he said. I would not have to stay overnight like most patients who had a tonsillectomy, because he was a doctor, he could look after me at home. This made me even happier. I remember feeling really lucky. But just as we were leaving the hospital room, that gray-haired nurse came in to say goodbye, and I felt the same sense of terror wash over me.

We left and got back into the Buick. My father was at the wheel, as before, but this time I sat in the back seat, right next to my mother. I remember her telling me I could eat plenty of ice cream to make my throat feel better. The terrible, scary day was over, or so I thought. But it wasn't actually gone from my mind.

Fast-forward to my teen and adult years: My career plans started to center on becoming a doctor, following in my father's and my uncle's footsteps. For several years after having my tonsils removed, I continued to have memories and flashbacks of that terrifying moment when the nurse grabbed me as we entered the hospital. It's important to point out, too, that I never had any bad feelings or thoughts about my surgeon father. He had figured out what I needed, and did his best to solve a medical problem for his only son.

Those were different times. Parenting styles change like anything else. A parent today would handle this kind of situation differently, offering explanations and reassurances about what was going to take place, perhaps staying with his child for as long as he could. But the thinking back then was just to get things over with. I don't think walking me through the whole procedure until I understood it would have been in my father's thoughts at that time, and I don't blame him for that. It's not easy to explain hospitals and surgery to a five- or six-year-old, and he probably thought he was sparing me from fears and worries.

Also, in truth, the ride to the hospital was not all that bad. Being in a car with my father was always a treat. My anxiety and subsequent terror really came from the way that one nurse had handled the situation. That's what really scared me. I think if she had said, "Hi there, how are you? Let me show you around," or offered me a toy—as is done today when you bring a tot into an emergency room—I would have felt reassured and comforted, and been able to handle whatever came next.

As a psychiatrist looking back on this experience, the question that interests me is what, if any, lasting trauma occurred from it? For a while I was hypersensitive even to *hearing* about hospitals, or people going into the hospital—and given my father's profession, it was frequently a topic of family conversations. I also had recurring visions—of this nurse grabbing me inside the hospital doorway, of her putting the anesthesia mask over my face.

I thought this through at about age eleven, when I made the decision to become a doctor. I remember making the clear decision that I could let go of these fears. Nothing bad had happened to me, after all. I was *fine*. Whether I already had some early inkling of what would years later become my LPA technique, I don't know. But I do remember thinking, "I don't have to be scared of this." And I also know I made a complete self-recovery. At least I thought so, until my first year as a psychiatric resident, after I'd finished medical school.

Dredging Up Old Memories

In the first year of training, which was mainly inpatient psychiatry, learning to treat patients, attending daily lectures, and having individual supervision, we also had a weekly group therapy session for all the trainees. This included residents from all the years of training, so it was a pretty big group, run by two psychiatrists. Part of the experience was not only learning about the group therapy process, but having a chance to discuss the stresses and problems of being a young doctor, and the emotional and practical issues we might encounter in treating patients. All in all, the intentions were good. It was not a bad thing to be able to talk like this.

But as time moved along, those sessions took on a different tone. The psychiatrists who led the group began to probe deeper into our personal lives, something I didn't think was right at the time and still think was inappropriate. We hadn't asked to be patients. In this case, we were being "psychoanalyzed"—you might even say scrutinized— in front of our peers, and it was not exactly comfortable.

 Each of us was asked to describe a frightening situation in our lives. Naturally, I referred back to my early trauma over that tonsillectomy. It was a memory, far in the past. But the two psychiatrists seized on it. They focused on my father, framing his behavior as thoughtless and even brutal—didn't I see how he had tricked me into going to the hospital? Didn't I realize I'd been manipulated, a child victimized by false pretenses?

Well, no, I said. Because I honestly didn't. My response was protective of my father. I took care to point out what a good father he was. I told the group and the two psychiatrists that every Wednesday afternoon, after he finished his surgery, he'd take me out of school an hour early and we'd go to a movie, a museum, a boat show, a car show or the planetarium. This started at around age five and went on until I was twelve, when I developed my own social life and could no longer leave school early. I also told them my father had bought me my first car, paid for my college, covered my medical school tuition. And he'd been my inspiration for choosing a medical career in the first place. He was my rock.

There were lots of other good things my father did as I grew up. But the psychiatrists did not listen. They countered every positive thing I said about him, insisting that it was "defensiveness," and that I was idealizing the man.

It was a no-win situation. A few of my fellow trainees began laughing at the way the psychiatrists kept pursuing this, but other than that, no one pointed out how these views were not even based on medically documented fact, but on personal theories. I remember bringing that up. One of the psychiatrists was so offended that he claimed these "theories," developed by great thinkers in the field (i.e., Freud and his followers) were *more accurate* than mathematics or physics. Didn't I know that? Half the group was laughing at his assertion, but we were trainees, after all. We were putty in their hands.

The negative thoughts these doctors were aiming to plant in my mind, and their attempts to undermine a great relationship, certainly had an effect on me. But I doubt it was the effect they'd intended. Instead of doubting myself and my feelings about my father, I began to doubt their approach. I should thank these two, actually, as they gave me a strong early start in avoiding that type of therapy. I was absolutely struck by how undermining it was. It was a therapeutic approach not focused on problem solving, but on creating more problems—by sowing the seeds of emotional dissent, and dredging up buried events from the past with their interpretations being guesswork at best.

My father was still alive and active in his surgical practice at that time, so I ran by him how these training psychiatrists were interpreting my tonsillectomy. He set me straight on several points. While we were in the car, he did tell I was going to a hospital to get my sore throats and earaches fixed and that a doctor I already knew would do the job—something I'd entirely forgotten. He also told me clearly that he would be with me the whole time, as he was a senior doctor at the hospital. And he reported that he had been furious at that nurse, whom he'd never felt good about.

Being an assertive surgeon, my father immediately asked, "Do you want me to go talk to these psychiatrists and set them straight with reality?" I assured him that wouldn't be necessary, that I could handle it, and furthermore, they do end up giving evaluations. He agreed, but added, "I wonder what kind of parents they are." I could see he was miffed at the questioning of his good intentions years earlier in my upbringing, and I was actually somewhat relieved to learn that he had informed me of what was going to happen. I knew my father was telling the truth, because that's the kind of person he was.

A Tale of Two Therapies

Unfortunately, so many people who seek help through therapy are met with that same kind of unproductive approach. In comparison, let's look at how one of my brilliant psychiatric colleagues, a down-to-earth, pragmatic practitioner of CBT, and how she responded. When I recounted that same story of the tonsillectomy, she did not fault my father, or argue with any kind of defensive response on my part. Instead, she made the more accurate observation that my teenage self could have benefited from a better understanding of the trauma I'd suffered, with recurrent images of that nurse. It was the nurse who had frightened me as a young child, with her startling face and her harsh bedside manner. Had the psychiatrists running that session listened a little more carefully, they might have been able to focus more on that.

We got to talking about this: even from the start, my colleague hadn't been taught that way. In her contemporary training program at a major teaching center, she told me that for at least two of her four years she was inundated by psychoanalytic/psychodynamic theories. And these, she noted, were presented as the major or even the *only* way to solve a person's problems or disorders. What upset her (and me) most is that so many therapists, including psychiatrists, psychologists, and the whole band of social workers and other practitioners, still continue to worship psychoanalytic notions put forth *more than a century ago*. The widespread allegiance to these antiquated and cult-like philosophies interferes with simply trying to improve patients' lives as simply and quickly as possible. No other field of medicine or health care can boast of this absurdity.

For example, a psychoanalyst or psychodynamic therapist would envision what would have been inferred to me if I'd been a patient in traditional psychodynamic therapy: that I was not *really* angry at the nurse. Instead, I'd have been told that the problem rested with my father, whom I idealized so much I couldn't bear to blame him for taking me to the hospital, instead displacing my unconscious anger at my father onto the nurse. My colleague further explained how I'd be accused of defending his actions, and placing him on a pedestal to counter my own feelings of helplessness and rage. In traditional psychoanalytical or psychodynamic parlance, she continued, I did this because I was compelled to see and preserve him as a "good object." These analytic and dynamic therapists see people as "objects" as they interpret and describe situations. I turned my father into an entity who could do no harm because to see him in any other way would be mentally intolerable. The worse his actions, the more I would feel compelled to defend and idealize him.

And then? Then the psychodynamic therapist would have led me to explore how much repressed rage lay behind this idealization, which I might be unable to express due to "castration anxiety." That's a loaded term, defined differently by a variety of analytic/dynamic thinkers, from the Freudian fear of losing your privates to a wider definition of your whole persona being taken away. So instead of expressing my rage at my father, I chose to identify with him instead, and became like him in my own behaviors and choices.

Looking at this today, this interpretation is almost laughable. But somehow, so many patients are still subjected to such analyses. It was like dipping a toe into a very bad agenda, in which the treatment itself can take a patient and hold him or her hostage to an antiquated, dangerous, altering sense of self.

From Talking to the Pharmacy

This stuff goes on and on. That therapeutic process can take many years—or for some psychoanalytic patients in the Woody Allen-movie mold, many *decades*—at tremendous expense, and let us not forget that expense is a key factor. Sometimes, in fact, you might get worse in reaction to certain unacceptable ideas your psychiatrist or therapist is insinuating. If you are seeing a psychiatrist, he or she might prescribe a medication as you fail to improve.

If you see a non-MD therapist, he or she may refer you to a prescribing psychiatrist or a primary care doctor to prescribe medications. As you continue to unravel these absurdities and unconscious configurations, it gets more and more costly and frustrating. All too often, the patient/client eventually makes some accurate assessment that the real problem is not being addressed, but is either assured that he is "getting there" or accused of "resisting the process." According to a Harvard study some years ago, over 50 percent of psychiatric patients will drop out of traditional talk therapy treatment, even though they claim to like their therapists.

But in a CBT program, or using my LPA technique, the process is entirely different. It's short, focused, and goal-oriented. Working with your therapist, you identify the mistaken ideas and distorted thoughts that led to some type of distress. Then you challenge these thoughts and exchange them for a more realistic perspective. This process allows you to develop and learn a new and better set of responses to the old set of problems—and those responses will continue to work when your treatment is over. The goal is not to meander all over your brain, probing the outdated beliefs and fantasies that a therapist is projecting onto you. The goal is to thoughtfully learn or relearn new techniques and perspectives to get your problem solved so you can find freedom fast.

CHAPTER 2

Stuck in a Pill Bottle with a Limited Book: The Other Problem with Psychiatry and Psychotherapy

We're all familiar with the cartoon archetype of the psychiatrist as a bearded man taking notes on a pad while his patient lies prone on the couch. But these days, the patient's more likely to be sitting upright in a chair, and the psychiatrist may well be writing a prescription, scrawling notes on a pad or typing into a computer. Psychopharmacology is the order of the day.

Got a problem? Take a pill. Doesn't work? Try a different pill, or add another pill to what you're already taking. The visit may be only fifteen or twenty minutes, and the newest term used for this type of care is "medication management."

Yes, your psychopharmacologist may eventually find a medication that makes you feel better, and that's a good thing. But medications treat symptoms, not what's causing the problem. And in order to keep feeling better, you need to keep taking the medication. For some patients, continued medication is essential, depending on what types of emotional disorders we are speaking about. But for many, it may not be.

What's in That Bottle

This book is not about psychopharmacology, but I will include a few observations about why many commonly prescribed meds are not as helpful as advertised. When it comes to treating anxiety disorders, the go-to medications for years were (and in many cases still are) the benzodiazepines, first sold commercially in 1960 as Librium (chlordiazepoxide) and followed a few years later by Valium (diazepam). Over the years, more types of benzodiazepines have been added to the original list. Ativan (lorazepam), Klonopin (clonazepam), and Xanax (alprazolam) are currently among the most popular.

Due to the addictive potential of these "benzos" and subsequent withdrawal issues, they are listed as controlled substances. In addition, benzodiazepines can be dangerous when combined with certain pain medications, including opiates. So, many clinicians are moving away from these anti-anxiety medications, even though in many circumstances they have proved to be helpful in treating anxiety, with careful observation and monitoring.

Recently some the SSRIs (selective serotonin reuptake inhibitors), long used in the treatment of depression, have been approved and used for the treatment of anxiety. The SSRI Prozac (fluoxetine) was introduced in 1987, later followed by Zoloft (sertraline), Paxil (paroxetine), Celexa (citalopram) and Lexapro (escitalopram). They are not controlled substances, and appear to be helpful for some anxiety patients, but many clinicians and consumers report that they are not as effective as the benzodiazepines.

Prescribing a pill is the way many people want to cure their problem, whether it's mental or physical. Many pharmaceutical products are truly life-saving, and can successfully treat a variety of mental and physical disorders and we should not forget that. Again, with certain severe depressions, bipolar type mood disorder and the schizophrenias, some medications are truly life-saving, allowing patients to lead productive lives. But when it comes to treating anxiety disorders—including post-traumatic stress syndrome, generalized anxiety, and phobias—the many variations of Cognitive Behavior Therapy, including my own LPA method, can be even more effective. That's because the approach is able to create lasting changes in how people think and respond. The patient develops the tools to come at the same old problem from a new perspective, and change the way he or she will behave.

Because so many medications are prescribed, one of the great problems in today's psychiatric and mental health care system is the tremendous overuse of medication with the mixing and matching of psychotropic medication all too often not designated for the intended treatment. It's not unusual to see a person taking three to five medications and not feeling any better, or even feeling worse from the multiple side effects. The lack of clear blood testing or imaging to detect psychiatric disorders leaves the diagnosis up to the clinician. All too often, subjective thinking, writing a prescription that's easy, pharmacological influences, or insurance reimbursement considerations can dominate the picture.

As I see it, the over diagnosis of bipolar disorder for irritability or moodiness and the widespread use of antidepressants for unhappy people who are not clinically depressed is something the psychiatric profession has yet to deal with adequately. And some experts who study mood disorders and depression have pointed out that more than half of those treated with antidepressants fail to respond to the medication.

When a pill's effects wear off, the problem remains. The only way to keep the problem at bay is to keep taking the pills. In some cases, getting off the pills can cause so much havoc to the brain chemistry that it creates even more problems for the patient.

Even mind-body problems, such as chronic insomnia, may respond better to CBT therapies. In 2016, the American College of Physicians recommended CBT as first-line treatment instead of medication for many adult patients with chronic sleeping difficulties. And in my own patients, when they are able to tackle and overcome a problem that's been keeping them up at night, guess what? They can get to sleep. *Without* the aid of a pill.

The *DSM* and Its Discontents

"You'll be pleased to know that no matter how long you have been neurotic, you will no longer be neurotic by 1980." That's how I opened one of my syndicated daily health care radio programs in the the late 1970s, one year before the *DSM-III* was introduced, reporting in this new version of the *DSM*, the word neurotic and its concept was dropped. *DSM* stands for *Diagnostic and Statistical Manual of Mental Disorders.* In reality, the *DSM-III* was a giant departure and an important step forward from the *DSM-II* of 1968, in that it worked very hard to define and list clusters of symptoms in the diagnosis of mental disorders. Over the years, leading up to the current *DSM-5*, this lends itself more and more to a biological model of mental disorders, with the subsequent use of increased medication in a medical field—psychiatry—where biological markers are still lacking, compared to other medical specialties.

Along with codification and classification, this tome is regularly used to diagnose patients, sending many down the path of medications. Although the *DSM* is a necessary resource to codify and classify mental disorders, its current biological leanings have unfortunately tried to medicalize many social experiences and normal human variations, affixing labels to many conditions that appear to be more subjective opinions and reasonable guesses.

The American Psychiatric Association (APA) first published the *DSM* in 1952 in order to control the variability of psychiatric diagnoses from one doctor to another. Theoretically, it's a good idea. Since it first came out, the book has gone through a series of updates, usually referred to by number: *DSM-II* (1968), *DSM-III* (1980), *DSM-III-R*

(1987), *DSM-IV* (1994), *DSM-IV-TR* (2000), and the most recent, *DSM-5*, published in 2013. For the latest edition, the APA finally dropped the Roman numerals—one update I think we can agree is a change for the better.

The *DSM's* website calls it "the standard classification of mental disorders used by mental health professionals in the U.S." A *DSM* diagnosis is a necessary requirement for most interactions with insurance companies, hospitals and clinics, pharmaceutical companies, lawyers and the court system. So you can see just how important these diagnostic definitions can be.

But that does not mean these definitions are always accurate. Nor are they comprehensive: in some cases, they leave out or misattribute key symptoms, because the *DSM's* diagnostic labeling is often simplistic and one-dimensional. It does not take into consideration such essential factors as a patient's environment, support system, or personality type in order to give an accurate assessment. We are all individuals—our lives, our emotions, our personalities, and how we may process information through our nervous systems are different. No two of us are the same, and each and every diagnostic label can differ from person to person.

Yet, while the *DSM's* accuracy is debatable, countless patients or clients of mental health professionals are nevertheless categorized by its standards—so much so that it's often referred to as the "bible" of psychiatric illnesses. But it is far from a bible of any sort. At best, it's a guidebook. Some have called it a dictionary, as it attempts to classify multiple mental disorders, but includes far more subjective thinking than scientific validation. It takes a top-down approach, using a checklist of symptoms in a one-dimensional manner, as opposed to a bottom-up assessment, which would look at the multiple factors in a person's life and background, and factor them as well as the symptoms, and then, on that, make a diagnosis.

Since I'm in the industry, so to speak, I use the *DSM*. I have to. I use it to procure the necessary insurance reimbursement for my patients, and at times, I've used it as an educational tool. It is a handy reference guide for teaching trainees, and it provides a framework in the areas of anxiety disorders, which include phobias, obsessive thoughts, some aspects of PTSD, and general anxiety disorder (called "neurosis" before the *DSM-III*, as noted above), which is what we're covering in this book. But it is not the definitive categorizer it presents itself to be. I think there are far too many patients who fall between the cracks, or are treated for the wrong issue, because they are labeled with a *DSM* diagnosis where the clinician fits them based on a checklist of symptoms, without factoring in the many facets of human behavior from person to person.

You can trace the subjectivity in the *DSM* through the shift in its format and information. The 1980 *DSM-III* introduced a more in-depth codifying system, labeling 265 types of psychiatric disorders. With each edition, that number has grown: there are 374 types of psychiatric disorders listed in the current *DSM-5*. But along with these changes and additions have come a great deal of controversy, particularly with the *DSM-III* and successive revisions. I'm not the only one who questions its scientific validity. Even as an instrument that aims to standardize and classify mental disorders, many feel the book has failed.

In the early days before the *DSM* existed, general practitioners, psychiatrists, and psychologists could easily disagree on a patient's diagnosis—that is true. But has that changed? Actually, it hasn't. If ten DSM-trained psychiatrists examine the same patient today, believe it or not, you may *still* get eight or ten different diagnostic labels. This kind of disagreement is not seen in general medicine or surgery, as a rule. Differing opinions do sometimes occur, but most often, for no more than one or two possibilities—usually referred to as a differential diagnosis.

Unlike the way medical diagnosis often works, the *DSM* format is a checklist. It does not include a multidimensional history of the symptoms, labs, imaging procedures (which, of course, do not exist yet) or possible causes of the disorder through biological mediators, or how each and every individual copes differently with these symptoms. All of these are key factors in making a good assessment and plotting a course of action in terms of care. But at the same time, as more labels are added with each new edition, the medicalization of many behaviors, some of which can be entirely within the range of normal, has entered the picture. And that's where medications come back in.

For example, the *DSM* has given a new label to temper tantrums: Disruptive Mood Dysregulation Disorder. Also, excessive eating (defined as more than twelve times in three months but not necessarily clinically adhered to) is now called Binge Eating Disorder and a medication has been approved for it, even though we are surrounded by great food and many Americans overeat as a matter of course. For most problem overeaters, a behavior modification program centered around eating disorders is probably more effective and longer lasting. But we now have a psychiatric label with limited studies or research offered to the public, so this behavior is advertised as a disorder. And guess what? Here's a pill to treat it.

The Over-Medication Epidemic

It's been suggested that the pharmaceutical industry is having a greater and greater influence on the minds of those creating the DSM. In recent years, we've seen "epidemics" of Attention-Deficit/Hyperactivity Disorder (ADHD) and childhood Bipolar Disorder, leading to frequent management by medication. This enhances the "Big Pharma" goals of prescribing medication to handle most mental disorders, even though many mental problems can be resolved by problem-focused variations of the "talking cure," and even more by CBT and my version, LPA.

Again, it's undeniably true that some severe mental illnesses, such as the schizophrenias, bipolar disorders, and clinical depression, respond well to medication and require ongoing medication for effective management. And with good medication management, we are all safer, healthier, and live longer lives due to the advances of pharmaceuticals. But it's also true that the need to expand and sell more products is an endless motivation for these corporate giants.

Here's another example: grief. The current *DSM-5* had planned to include grief, or bereavement, as a depressive disorder. That would have allowed primary care physicians (who by the way prescribe well over 50 percent of psychotropic medications) to incorporate bereavement as a medicinally managed disorder. In other words, if you were grieving, they might have prescribed a pharmaceutical cure. So much for going through a natural and healthy process of experiencing and processing loss.

Luckily, the outcry against this wrongheaded classification was so intense that it was dropped from the new *DSM-5*. And behavioral addictions, such as "Sex Addiction," "Exercise Addiction," and "Shopping Addiction" also proved controversial and are not included in the new *DSM*, although many on the *DSM-5* panels would have loved to slap a diagnostic label on what might be normal life experiences or choices, based more on personal opinions than any sound medical/psychiatric basis. The major mental disorders have yet to be validated by biological testing, and it's disheartening to realize that the labels above that were proposed for the new *DSM-5* would have been listed as disorders without scientific validation. To think that many Americans, who are easily persuaded to shop by advertisers and go on shopping sprees when their finances allow it, could be subjectively labeled with a mental disorder defies common sense.

All of this has come to the attention of the National Institute of Mental Health (NIMH), which has made it clear that the new *DSM-5* is more a dictionary than a "bible" of disorders. The *DSM* offers a common terminology; its weakness, according to the past NIMH director, Dr. Thomas Insel, is validity. *DSM* diagnoses are based on clusters of symptoms, not on any laboratory measures, as in general medicine.

Of course, creating a system of biomarkers, as we have in other fields of medicine, is not currently possible. There's simply not enough data available yet on mental functioning at the biological level. There are no blood tests, X-rays or infallible tests to refer to when it comes to describing and codifying mental disorders. In the future, that will change: The NIMH has set up the Research Domain Criteria (RDoC) to help transform diagnosis by using genetics, imaging, and cognitive science, with the goal of developing a new classification system.

As pointed out by Bruce Cuthbert, PhD, director of the RDoC Unit at the NIMH in Bethesda, Md., the *DSM* sees single disorders or disease entities as the same for each patient, thus eliminating any exploration of variations with disorders or common mechanisms across disorders. Dr. Cuthbert further points out that results with neuroimaging, behavioral science, and genetics were inconsistent where similar patterns were frequently observed in multiple disorders, a situation attributed to diverse elements or variations, concurrent illnesses with other disorders and overspecification of the single dimensional categories. The emphasis for treatment with RDoC is to aim at specific impairments or target symptoms such as sleep difficulties or cognitive disturbances, just listing two as an example, similar to what most clinicians do in treatment settings where, as I see it, environmental factors, family and cultural support systems, and underlying personality styles play a part in diagnosis and treatment plans.

Science will advance, and we will learn more. But that's in the long term. Hopefully, it will go a long way toward correcting the oversimplification the *DSM* now encourages when making a diagnosis. But for now, we have only the *DSM-5* as our guide.

What this means is that we need humility and open-mindedness in diagnosis and treatment. True, the *DSM* is all we have, but this fallible guide has far too much influence over methods of labeling and subsequent methods of treatment.

Same Problems, Different Approach

But fortunately, responsible clinicians do continue to use their own medical judgment to assess, evaluate, and treat mental disorders in a multidimensional manner. That means taking a detailed history, considering individual responses and adaptations, and including some biological, sociological, and learned factors and issues into an effective treatment plan. Irritability and daily mood swings cannot be simply logged in as a bipolar disorder, the current "diagnosis du jour," just to satisfy an insurer and support the use of medications. There is no reason to medicate someone for simply being frustrated or unhappy if they don't meet certain well-established clinical criteria for depression or a mood disorder.

As you'll see in the case studies that follow, mistaking PTSD for pure depression, which may be one aspect of PTSD (to cite just one example of many) may lead to prescribing a useless cocktail of medications that do nothing to fix the problem or underlying the symptoms. Finding the proper therapy is not simple. What may work for one patient may not work for another. Psychopharmacology isn't a magic bullet, as we have learned in treating depression, where often one or more medications may fail. Neither are psychodynamic therapies that meander around and around with no fixed goal in sight. But the CBT techniques of the great Dr. Aaron Beck have demonstrated excellent results in treating many forms of depression. His techniques also work as well as for many people who struggle with commonly seen problems—including phobias, anxiety, and often-unrecognized forms of PTSD—neither medications nor psychodynamic therapies are completely effective in helping to solve the problem. Let's take a look at how some LPA treatments have worked—and how they may work for you.

CHAPTER 3

LPA in a Nutshell

So how does this work? I'm going to take you through the nuts and bolts of my Learning, Philosophizing, and Action technique. It's a three-part, short-term, cognitive therapy program that I expanded from a practical way to achieve smoking cessation and weight control into a short-term goal-oriented therapy that can effectively solve many kinds of problems. Though my LPA technique clearly goes beyond the one or two visits needed for smoking and weight control, it remains a short-term, goal-oriented method for problem resolution. I call it LPA because that's how it happens: you Learn, you Philosophize about what you learned and how it's affected you, and then you take Action to leave that behavior behind and move on with your life.

Some patients who come into my office don't ask me to explain anything. They're so bent on fixing the problem that they dive right into the process without any questions, ready to get right to work. Some have gone through previous therapies that focused on "what did you do this week?" and "what did that mean to you?" or "how did you feel about that?" even though their reasons for starting therapy originated from something specific: a phobia such as fear of elevators, crippling anxiety about catching the flu, fears about losing a job, or obsessive flashbacks of a car accident. They sit down. "Doc," they say, "fix me."

Other patients want to know every detail. They want to take the time to analyze what everything means, to grasp the theory behind it. We're all different: we're wired differently; we learn differently. The "hardware" in our brains, are mostly the same, but the "software" put in over the years is quite different for each of us. For those who learn best by example, there are plenty of examples in this book that will *show* you how LPA works. In the chapters ahead, you'll read detailed examples of different people with different personality structures and different problems to solve. But for people who ask for a simple explanation of how LPA works, and because we need to establish what's known in therapy-speak as a baseline, here are the three basic phases.

Phase One: Learning

In the first session or two, we discuss the problem that brought you here. Though the scope of discussion is tailored to each individual patient, we keep the focus on the problem you want to solve and talk about how the behavior in question may have been learned. My aim is to help you recall something that actually happened: When did you learn this behavior, develop this attitude about yourself or about the world? Who taught you to think this way? The learned material, i.e., the "software" that your brain is using, may have been full of fears or negativity. It may have been inconsistent, or promoted bad behaviors as positive experiences, thus affecting your future thinking, situations, and responses. In a nutshell: What tape has your brain been playing?

A simple example of faulty learning would be teaching a small child that 2+2=3. In the first day or two of school, the teacher turns that around with the simplest re-learning techniques that will last a lifetime. Clearly, it's more difficult to alter faulty learned beliefs and perspectives, but it's very doable, and our brains have the ability to accomplish that as long as we are motivated for change.

Phase Two: Philosophizing

In the next few sessions, we focus on what we now know. We work on extrapolating the behavior that you've learned. We move from specific memories to a larger view, so that we can recognize the origins of this behavior, whether it be learned fears, insecurities, or negative judgments like "you'll never be able to do that." We look at how those flawed, faulty, unfounded messages and beliefs, many times not done purposely but unwittingly, you got from your family and others have affected you—as a child, then becoming an adult, still stuck with these faulty beliefs. How does this thinking affect your behavior in the present? How has it affected the decisions and choices you've made?

In a nutshell: How did that tape get into my brain, and what effect is it having on me? How could I look at this differently so I can change the channel?

Phase Three: Action

Now it's time to unlearn those behaviors, through a structured thinking process that's also known as *cognition*. This is where our work—based on Cognitive Behavior Therapy— departs most directly from traditional talk therapy. We don't start exploring and ruminating, or expanding. Instead, we focus. We ask: What are you doing to overcome this? And we use some practical behavior modification techniques and Cognitive Behavior Therapy strategies, (or re-thinking strategies) coupled with basic relaxation and breathing exercises, visualization and split-screen techniques, reciprocal inhibition, in vitro flooding, progressive exposure, and hypnosis.

If some of these sound like difficult technical terms, don't worry. You'll get to see them in practical action throughout the following chapters, and learn how use each of them, separately or in combination, which can be used to unlock rigid thinking and make positive changes.

Think of these different techniques as a toolkit. My job is to figure out which of these tools will work best to get the job done. Separately, or in combination, they are designed to give you:

- a new set of perspectives on an old set of beliefs and problems
- the chance to succeed by applying a new set of thoughts and beliefs, such as getting over a phobia, giving up a self-destructive habit, or changing a troubling personality style.

The patient is taking *action*: thinking through and discussing well-thought-out activities—including the relaxation and visualization techniques listed above—inside the therapist's office, as well as in the outside world. These new, conscious behaviors produce a very positive personal reward: success in areas that previously were not working well.

In a nutshell: Now I can change the tape to something I want for my life.

The Big Picture

Why does LPA work? Because when a person does something successfully a number of times, the success-producing behaviors become more and more a part of who you are. They turn your thought and behavior patterns in a positive, productive direction. Instead of a locked-in response to a what-if fear that's become so ingrained it seems like an inescapable fact, you can look at it from a fresh perspective and see how unlikely it actually is. If you've built up a wall of reasons why something can't possibly change, you can take down that all-or-nothing thinking, brick by brick. You've taught your brain to respond in more positive ways and to take action to change your life.

How long does all of this take? It depends on the problem. It might take six or eight sessions over the course of two or three months. Sometimes even less. We're working with small numbers here.

It only takes a couple of sessions to understand how faulty, learned attitudes affect present-day actions and thoughts, and reinforce a lifetime of behaviors. Once we learn the source of the behavior, we acknowledge its impact. Having acknowledged its impact on you, you come to understand where your present-day behavior comes from. The past is affecting your present. But it doesn't have to. That's the big revelation: you're in control.

Once you've accomplished this change of perspective, we take action to change the behavior that's stood in your way, so you can move on with your life. That's the goal. We are not going to dig so profoundly into your personality structure and history that it will take years to come out of that deep, dark mine. We're going to help you to find freedom fast.

PART ONE

Phobias

CHAPTER 4

The Nature of Fear

Don't drive into the tunnel ... The dog's going to bite ... Patients have described their phobias to me as walking around with the devil on their shoulder or a voice inside their head that just won't stop. Whether temporarily self-defeating or utterly crippling, phobias can get hold of us and seem to take over. Your neighbor's sweet Golden Retriever turns into a dangerous monster that's going to turn on you and bite. The short plane ride is going to turn into an epic crash. The elevator's going to snap off its cables. The spider in the corner is going to leap off the wall and attack. The car is going to veer left and into oncoming traffic—even though you've got both hands on the wheel and your eyes on the road. And to certain poor souls, germs are everywhere, sickness is everywhere, and they have no choice but to wear gloves wherever they go, even in the heat of summer.

A phobic response is as an irrational, persistent fear of an object, a particular situation, or a type of circumstance. It's paralyzing, overwhelming, and self-perpetuating. Once you're in its grip, it's very hard to shake it on your own. You may or may not know where you got such notions: you never consciously decided any of it. But there it is, going on in your mind: a phobia you can't shake.

Why? Because a phobia is the result of more than just a momentary scary thought or two. It may start as a moment, but it grows into a learned, automatic thought, which leads to certain repeated behaviors. The phobia *itself* creates a huge amount of anxiety, and therefore, you tend to avoid its source: if you're afraid of bees, you just don't go near them. But here's what's really going on: what you're *really* working to avoid is not the bees, it's the way being near bees makes you *feel*. Of course, the more you feed that fear, the more you avoid it, the more you reinforce the phobia, and it's not about bees at all anymore. It's about being phobic of bees.

So you're now supporting the neurons in your brain that keep you from going near bees. You're wiring your brain to have a very specific pattern of avoiding the phobia, and telling it, essentially, *you're right*. The brain *learns* that what's most important in this hierarchy is avoidance. In phobias, in particular, this learning becomes hardwired.

Phobias cause a huge amount of anxiety—and they're incredibly common. They cause people to drastically change their daily routines, scale back plans, ambitions, and goals. They affect everything, from our jobs to our relationships, from what we eat and how we sleep to how often we get sick. The stress they can produce is crippling—but so, too, can be the sense of hopelessness they generate. When they go untreated, the resulting stress and anxiety can become so severe that additional psychiatric disorders can occur, such as bouts of heavy depression, other forms of anxiety, and, of course, substance abuse. Having just experienced a flash of utter terror, it's entirely common to want to have a drink. But that in itself can magnify into a pattern, until just the *thought* of having to do something is enough to trigger a thirst.

I've treated many, many patients successfully for all sorts of phobias. I've seen some remarkable ones: germophobia, a phobia of getting sick during flu season, cockroach phobia (big in New York City), cat phobia, pigeon phobia, a phobia of catching a foot condition from trying on shoes in a shoe store. They're treatable because phobias don't necessarily need medication or long commitments to deep analytical discussions in talk therapy (like the "tell me about when you were five" approach to being afraid of driving.) But phobias do need treatment. To escape a phobia requires careful and deliberate work. Often, the results-oriented, matter-of-fact, collaborative LPA technique works extremely well.

LPA: Reversing the Pattern

The reason LPA is so effective is that it's a short-term but direct course of treatment. It progressively works to reverse what's a wired pattern by adding new software, in a sense. It's based on a learning theory: since you're constantly learning to avoid something, you can also learn to not avoid it just as well. When you start desensitizing yourself to just what you're so afraid of, you start breaking that chain. It takes practice, to be sure. But soon you're on the road to getting better.

For the sake of understanding, it's always good to know the basic framework of what ails you. I'm including this quick explanation of the clinical definitions of phobias, but keep in mind that these explanations are academic and not geared to helping an individual. You don't need to understand them, or even agree with them, in order to tackle and overcome your own phobia.

The truth is that the *DSM* (*Diagnostic and Statistical Manual of Mental Disorders*) is revised with every new edition as standard approaches change; we're now on the *DSM-5*. There's always some debate as to how to categorize phobias, but these three categories are routinely accepted:

Agoraphobia, a generalized fear of being in a place or open space where, if something happens, you may not get any help.

Social phobia, where a person is fearful and easily embarrassed of being in public and social situations where attention will be on them, such as public speaking, giving a paper, or performing.

Specific phobias, including situational phobias (such as being afraid of riding in elevators, flying on planes, being in enclosed spaces); natural phobias (such as being afraid of heights, storms, water, germs); and animal phobias (such as fear of dogs, cats, bugs, snakes). There are countless examples — including some that are incredibly rare and surprising. But if there's something to be phobic of, someone will be phobic. That's what I've learned in my long career as a psychiatrist.

Here's a list of the common phobias:
Acrophobia, fear of heights
Agoraphobia, fear of open spaces
Ailurophobia, fear of cats
Arachnophobia, fear of spiders
Claustrophobia, fear of enclosed spaces
Cynophobia, fear of dogs
Glossophobia, fear of public speaking
Hemophobia, fear of blood
Hydrophobia, fear of water
Mysophobia, fear of germs and dirt
Nyctophobia, fear of the dark
Ophidiophobia, fear of snakes
Pyrophobia, fear of fire
Triskaidekophobia, fear of the number 13
Trypanophobia, fear of injections and needles
Xenophobia, fear of strangers
Zoophobia, fear of animals

Of all of these, specific phobias are not only the most plentiful, they're also the most common. According to the National Institute of Mental Health, as of 2005, about 19 million people, 8.7 percent of the U.S. population had a specific phobia, and of those, some 32 percent were seeking treatment. In 2014 the Anxiety and Depression Association of America came up with the same stat—8.7 percent of the U.S. population—and found that phobias occurred twice as often in women as in men.

Certainly, all this is interesting, but I wonder about that other 68 percent who did not seek treatment. Why not? Perhaps if they knew there was an effective way of dealing with their fear and anxiety, they would have sought it out. Because, regardless of a phobia's origin, it can probably be treated with LPA.

Where Phobias Come From

For the sake of understanding, and because the mind is an amazing mechanism, here's the theoretical breakdown for the three possible origins for phobias. But again, let me emphasize, not only for the sake of common sense, but for therapeutic reasons: these are all academic. And as I've said before, the definitions in psychology and psychiatry often change and shift.

Learned. We all have fears, some based on experiences that we are conscious of, and some we cannot explain without psychological help. How do we create these fears and phobias? There must be some cause for something that can scare us so intensely. In actuality, many learning experiences can create these fears and phobias after we are exposed to these situations. They're aptly framed under the term *associative learning:* the learning experience, or event, that caused the phobia.

The associative learning links a usually fairly neutral situation, such as driving, petting a dog, or talking in front of an audience, with an entirely not neutral outcome. For instance, while driving, you have a terrible moment of panic on the road. Or that sweet dog suddenly snaps at you. Or, as you're speaking, something awkward and embarrassing occurs. Now sharp anxiety sets in. And suddenly, you have something to avoid. When you avoid the situation—and consequently the anxiety that set in as a result—you're now in phase 2 of the phobia, avoidance learning.

By its very nature, avoidance learning negatively reduces the anxiety: you don't do X or go to Y, and *that's* what creates the long-term phobia. Unhappy with how things have worked out or not (especially, say, if you had really enjoyed driving until that fateful day), you'll keep avoiding that object or situation long after the pivotal event. That's the only way you can also avoid feeling not only that surge of anxiety, but also the mental and physical stress that it triggers. So a pattern develops, and deepens, and the phobia becomes consolidated into a far larger behavior. It becomes part of you.

Genetic. A fascinating study on mice done in 2013 found that phobias can indeed be passed from generation to generation. Researchers exposed mice to the scent of cherry blossoms along with an electric shock. When the mice reproduced, their offspring also responded fearfully to the odor, though they had never been exposed to it or, to an accompanying shock. Even if the mice were fathered via artificial insemination, the same effect continued. And researchers found that structural changes had taken place in the brains of parent mice. Moreover, there were clear chemical changes in the animal's DNA as well. The findings suggest that certain experiences can be transferred from the brain into the genome, allowing them to be passed on to later generations. Is this a type of survival mechanism? A lot more work is being done to clarify this research.

There have also been studies of twins showing that even when raised in entirely different environments, the siblings will have the same phobia in later life. Interestingly, this is especially true for identical twins with social phobias. And some studies of people who suffer from specific phobias find that up to 66 percent of sufferers have at least one first-degree relative—a parent, child, or sibling—with the same specific phobia. This is especially true for people with a phobia of needles and injections (trypanophobia).

Psychoanalytic. I am a psychiatrist. That said, when I'm asked about the psychoanalytic origins of phobias, I usually start with a qualifier: Psychoanalysis is not a science. It's a theory or multiple theories put together over a hundred years ago by a number of great thinkers in the early days of modern awareness of mental health issues. The intentions were good, the theories very convincing and with no other courses of treatment available, intellectually it made sense. However, all too often, the ideas are accepted as universal truths without study or validation. If these ideas and theories are what work for you, and they may work for some, so be it, but it will take a long time to see results, if ever.

Let's see how it works.

The psychoanalytic theory of phobias is based largely on theories of repression and displacement. The belief is that phobias are symptoms, the byproduct of something far deeper: unresolved conflicts in our brain between our id (primitive responses) and our superego (conscience).

Psychoanalysts generally believe that the conflict began in childhood, and was either repressed or displaced onto the feared object. So the *object* of the phobia is not the original source of the anxiety. Which means your phobia about catching the flu from a subway staircase railing is actually not about germs, or the flu, or even the railing, at all. And your phobia of getting sick from eating in a restaurant is not really about the restaurant. Just because you actually did get sick (and therefore developed what you might *think* is a learned phobia) doesn't mean a thing. Really, a psychoanalyst might say, your fear of vomiting has to do with something that happened long, long ago, when you were a child.

Such analytic concepts have dominated psychiatric thinking for well over a century, and to some extent these theories and their modifications still do. My problem is that these complicated and speculative theories dominate certain treatment situations without having any real basis in any reliable scientific research. From where I sit, treating patient after patient, it has always been difficult to imagine a phobia in the here and now, regarding driving, elevators, or of dogs as the manifestation of one's anxiety for having unconscious incestuous thoughts toward a parent that got displaced into the current phobia. In the early days of these theories, the power of the analytic movement was so overwhelming that it was nearly impossible to challenge them. But to a behaviorist or learning theorist, they truly seemed off base.

Luckily, today, there is far more openness in our understanding and knowledge. Therapy has expanded to include successful short-term treatments that use the learned model emphasizing CBT and it's variants, behavior modification and guided imagery. And the fact that these treatments are a success has pushed back against this antiquated theory. Still, these theories are in use in far too many therapeutic situations, phobias among them.

CHAPTER 5

How LPA Conquers Your Phobia

Everyone's phobia is different. There's no one specific, single magic bullet that will make it go away. But usually, there is a *results-oriented* way to make it stop. What I have found works best is a combination of relaxation techniques, systematic desensitization and gradual, guided exposure—what you might call "reciprocal inhibition"—in which we counter the anxiety and stress caused by your phobic thoughts with pleasant visualizations. That's the LPA framework. Within that, the specifics depend entirely on the individual and the nature of the phobia.

Defusing the Fear

LPA involves working first *in vitro* (in your head), and then *in vivo* (in real life). With phobias, the *in vitro* phase involves gaining an understanding of the nature of the phobia: learning about it, then examining it from different points of view, philosophizing about it, considering it from different angles. Then we practice systematically desensitizing you with what I call *reciprocal inhibition*. This is a fancy term for the act of pairing the source of your anxiety with some kind of reaction that actually *reduces* that anxiety, therefore disconnecting the source from its effect on you.

The *in vivo* phase involves exposure to what scares you. And that may happen in gradual, even infinitesimal increments, as you'll see in the case about the man who was terrified of dogs. Sometimes the work produces a breakthrough that seems sudden, but is not, as with the lawyer who had to get over her fear of bridges and tunnels: suddenly, there she was, driving without hesitation across the George Washington Bridge. At the same time, or in whatever sequence the patient is comfortable with, he or she is also practicing on their own. I'll give some examples of that, too.

I've seen many people improve markedly, overcoming all sorts of phobias, using this system. Not only does the system itself work to modify the behavior, it also works to give patients a sense of faith in themselves, and a belief that they have the power to overcome their problem. If you are involved in your own improvement, it's a great feeling—you're investing time and effort in yourself. You are taking control of an issue that has a life of its own, involved and committed to a process that will be successful. In fact, it's a rare case in which someone *doesn't* improve—and I'll get to that—because success in treatment depends far more on the patient's own efforts than you've been led to believe.

Here's the truth: *The more motivated the patient, the better the outcome.* Perhaps, if we acknowledged that, our overreliance on paternalistic talk therapy, with its endless second-guessing and analysis, and on pharmaceuticals that all too often wreak havoc on brain chemistry and have all manner of unfortunate side effects, would be far less prevalent. Instead, we'd tackle many of our problems with specific, goal-oriented, targeted, short-term solutions, using the powers within ourselves, which is what this book is all about: feeling better faster.

A Gradual Process

What I do with LPA is gradually, step by step and at a pace that is comfortable with the patient, work to defuse the phobia. It is not a complicated method. It mimics the way we learn, as children, *not* to be afraid of something: by looking at it, examining it, deciding it's not really that scary at all, and then just accepting it as part of life. But here's a glimpse of the things I might cover with a patient. This is generic; each approach is tailored to each individual, but this is the general framework of how it works.

Relax

We start with some relaxation exercises to settle the mind and calm the nerves. That's important; you can't be doing this kind of work in an agitated state. I teach relaxation, and then you'll be able to do this on your own as you progress.

There are many relaxation techniques available. The one I prefer is the the eye-roll technique developed by Drs. Herbert and David Spiegel. It is easily teachable.

Learn

In the learning phase, I ask different types of questions. They're all geared to getting a general picture of a patient and his or her phobia. What often happens is patients gain insights as they answer the questions. This isn't some kind of manipulative questioning—I'm not trying to trick or outmaneuver anyone into focusing on any deeply buried thoughts hiding somewhere in their unconscious. LPA is a straightforward approach, which patients find reassuring.

Among the questions I might ask:

- What's your fear?
- How long have you felt this way?
- Does this fear have a physical effect on you? For instance, does it make your chest feel tight or your stomach knot up? Do you start sweating, does your heart beat faster? Do you feel an urge to go to the bathroom? Have you ever spontaneously eliminated during phobic anxiety?
- Does this fear have an impact on the way you act? Does it make you want to run away, or cause you to make excuses for your thoughts or behaviors?
- Did anyone else in your family have this phobia or a similar fear?
- Growing up, did you feel a lot of anxiety and stress in the house? Or did home feel safe and secure? Do you think you might have been somehow taught to fear certain things, and if so, which might you have been taught to fear?
- What about the people around you, your friends, people you met? Were you taught that people were essentially good, reliable, and trustworthy?
- What about things such as machines? Were you taught they were reliable and safe? And what about animals or insects? Did anything happen as you were growing up that made you believe they were unsafe and dangerous?
- What's your relationship with your family like now?
- How do you feel about yourself? Does the phobia affect your self-esteem, slow down your career advancement, hinder your social life, or affect your family and friends?
- These questions are a guide and not part of a rigid formula, and can vary and be expanded or contracted based on some of the answers.

Philosophize

As we start the philosophizing phase, we look back at your answers, and to the discussion that those answers generated. From there, we start painting a picture of you and your fears. The idea is to embark on a very basic, simple change of perspective, which will be a big step toward how you think about yourself and your phobia. It's a way of expanding your point of view about what's bothering you and a different way to think about things. We talk about any possible trends or patterns, and we might talk about what it's like to live with this particular fear: how it affects your daily life, your routines, your relationships, your choices.

Perhaps you'll remember something about the way you grew up that made you more anxious as a child. Maybe some part of you actually feels more comfortable with a certain level of stress—you've become so accustomed to it that it feels like a part of you. Or maybe it turns out that certain things trigger it the same way, such as being late, having a messy house, or misplacing something. It could be anything (and I've seen nearly everything).

Or perhaps you grew up thinking that anxiety was normal, which actually is a common characteristic for many phobia patients: they *learned* to be phobic. That's a faulty premise, and it's faulty learning, but it was learning, nonetheless. And once you know that, you can start to unlearn it.

The idea is to talk about it, and see what comes up, but not forever; not for months; not to the point where we're ignoring the reason you came in. We're not going to start trying to fix *everything*. We're only going to fix your phobia. So I might start doing what is another part of philosophizing, what I call the *possible versus probable* scenario. Most anxieties, panic, fears, phobias, and apprehensions are not only caused *by* flawed learning, they also *cause* flawed reasoning.

Consider these possibilities and probabilities:

It's certainly *possible* for the elevator to crash, or the plane to nose-dive, or the bridge to collapse, but is it *probable*?

There is certainly a possibility that the world might end tonight while you sleep, but is it probably going to happen?

That mosquito on the wall may indeed turn around and somehow manage to bite you before you smash it with your newspaper, but will it?

The old cat that is napping in a sunny spot on your friend's bed as you sit in your friend's living room and have tea may *possibly* wake up, go directly to you, and scratch you hard. But it's sleeping, and it's been sleeping for hours. So do you think it's actually going to get up from its warm spot in the sunshine, see that you in particular are in the house, and unsheathe its claws to attack you?

Probably not.

Once you start considering the odds, you can start dialing back your fear.

Doing this kind of homework and working out this kind of thought process has incredible value to the person doing it. You're facing the subject of your fear, you're taking it upon yourself to think *rationally* and learn something about your fear, and you are probably going to find that it is really not that bad. I've had my patients research statistics on everything from insect bites to car crashes to dog attacks to building collapses to snakebites to elevator mishaps—and then work on extrapolating the probability. Nearly every time, they are pleasantly surprised, and that surprise turns to relief. Nothing like real information to quell a rumor, right? Admittedly, there are those few who want help but focus on the "yes, buts" to almost any new idea. However, with a bit more time and motivation, help is waiting for them.

One woman said to me, "It's amazing what a little dose of reality can do when you think it through without an emotional charge." The phobic response in based on a type of all-or-nothing thinking, for example:

The dog will bite me, so if I stay away from the dog, it won't bite me.

As we develop a new kind of thinking, a new perspective develops:

Well, it does seem like although some (though very few) dogs bite, and some dogs seem a bit difficult to deal with, most dogs are gentle, and completely enjoy being around people. They even like people. Given the chance, they'll wag their tails and lick your hand.

As this new thinking takes root, the concept of possibilities and probabilities increases, and a broader view of the phobia occurs.

With a phobia, the terrible possibilities run like a tape loop in your head. Without anyone countering them, they just keep looping and replaying. But instead, stop and ask yourself: what are the chances? *What are the chances this happens?* That's all it takes.

There are many ways to ask yourself this. One approach is to list the pros and cons of the very thing you're afraid of, such as an airplane. Another is to carefully examine the positives and negatives of giving up your phobia. Forecast the outcome for yourself: If I give up this fear, what will be easier, and what will be harder? Here's an example laid out in a chart. I often encourage my patients to do this. It has a way of laying out just how probable your phobia actually is—in black and white.

Elevator Phobia: Possible Versus Probable

Possibility	Probability
I could get stuck in the elevator.	In all the years I did ride elevators (which was until three years ago), I never once got stuck in one.
If I did get stuck in an elevator with strangers, we could be stuck in there for days.	Not only have I never been stuck on an elevator, but the elevators I did take all had an intercom or an alarm buzzer, so we could certainly make the problem known — and not be stuck for days at all.

I could die stuck in an elevator, with no one knowing I'm there.	This is an extremely rare event. And, again, I know elevators do have all sorts of emergency systems to call for help. Plus, I have my cell phone.
I could be so scared I had a heart attack.	No one in my family has ever had a heart attack. Also, I get regular physical checkups. So I have to admit this is not a strong possibility at all.

Chances are, as you ask yourself these questions, there will be a reflexive response going on, which I call the "Yes, But…" response. Work on keeping that *Yes, But* out of your own internal conversation with yourself. Consider that the voice of a very negative non-friend, who is not on your side. Give it an identity of sorts. One patient of mine even had a nickname for his. He called it his "pinhead," a voice that was always trying to cast doubts and negative feelings when he was doing his best to work his way out of them. "It's as if this pinhead of a voice *wants* me to feel bad," he said. "But I'm not going to let him."

Throughout this book, I'm going to bring up one key to LPA: the patient. LPA is a participatory therapy. It's up to the patient to practice and do the work. It's about action.

Elevator Phobia: Easier/Harder

Let's look at another example. It's someone considering their own elevator phobia, using the easier/harder exercise, and it's taken from work I did (successfully) with a patient:

What will be easier	What will be harder
I won't waste as much time because I can simply ride the elevator and not have to climb the stairs.	I'll have to figure out a reason that explains to my staff and co-workers why I take the stairs.
I'll arrive at meetings without being all sweaty from running up the stairs.	I won't have to explain why I'm out of breath before a meeting.
I won't always feel so inadequate and neurotic because of my fear.	I will have to figure out how to distract myself when I am forced to take an elevator.
I'll feel far more in control of myself and my thoughts.	I won't be able to blame losing a client or having a bad meeting on my phobia anymore.

What often happens in this philosophizing phase is that reason takes over. And in some cases, it's a tremendous surprise. "Is that true?" a patient once exclaimed, as if he had just suddenly discovered an incredible secret. It was as if he'd just realized he held the key to unlocking this trap he'd been in for years. The key was common sense.

CHAPTER 6

Overcoming Phobias With LPA: Real Stories

Let's look at some examples of phobias now. As with all the examples I write about in this book, I've changed the names, merged, and combined case histories and some telling details to protect the patients. But the process they went through, and the emotions and reactions they had are entirely real. After reading these stories, you will see that the proper treatment is helpful.

Phobia Case Study #1: Joyce Crosses the Bridge

Among one of the most interesting aspects to being a psychiatrist is the incredible paradox that phobias create in people. A person can be fully functioning, successful, even a star in his or her field. He or she can have a great marriage or a lovely relationship, can raise children and be a pillar of the community, can be an amazing performer or singer or innovator, and yet be privately stricken with an utterly crippling, terrifying, paralyzing phobia.

If it's a specific kind of phobia, most of the time friends, coworkers, and family members won't even know. It also depends on the phobia: in some cases, the fear affects the way a person functions in daily life to such an extent that it's obvious to others. In other cases, it's a painful secret, something to be struggled with in private.

Another aspect I'm fascinated with is what happens when someone in this position seeks therapy. All too often, it's the wrong kind of therapy, and this is a troubling subject to me. Frequently the therapy is either in a psychoanalytic or psychodynamic mode, or it involves pharmaceuticals, or both.

By the time Joyce came to me, she had already found out that the anti-anxiety medication she had been prescribed (frequent anti-anxiety medications include Valium or Klonopin) made her very tired. The antidepressants now used for anxiety and phobias (such as Prozac, Paxil, or Zoloft) made her feel really sick. So now she was searching for a treatment without medications.

Joyce had already been to a variety of psychotherapists, but to no avail. Why? As I recall her telling me, they treated her phobia as a representation of a deeper-seated issue, making a psychoanalytic/psychodynamic mountain out of a pretty specific situation. She was directed at the deeper meaning of her phobia as it related to unresolved conflicts of childhood and even adulthood that were now displaced into her specific phobia. And when she told a therapist she really just wanted to figure a way out of her phobia, she was told that she was trying to control her treatment as a result of being afraid to face those unresolved, mysterious, as yet-unidentified.... You get the picture.

So instead, she came to me. Joyce was terrified of driving through tunnels or on bridges. That was her problem, and it was serious, potentially career-ending. She was a successful divorce attorney, and because of where she lived, and her work, she had to take tunnels and bridges all the time. A large part of her work time was spent hauling heavy folders and boxes of critical, time-sensitive documents between the offices of colleagues, her own office, and court. Her job entailed an endless and mandatory round-robin of the kind of stops a busy lawyer has to make, and there was no way to avoid bridges and tunnels. So every trip she took was fraught with terror.

Joyce was one tough cookie. She clearly had inner strength. But she was discouraged and pessimistic by the time she walked into my office, and she let me know this. She told me in no uncertain terms that she wasn't interested in an in-depth analysis of theories relating to a fear of being abandoned or some kind of mother issues, or the nonsense of unresolved who-knows-what-feelings from childhood. She was disgusted with the frustrating sessions she'd had with a battery of other psychotherapists. Intellectually, she explained, she understood her problem: an irrational, persistent fear of crossing bridges and going through tunnels, but she had no idea how to overcome it. Her attitude was almost challenging: *Fix the problem I need you to fix*.

"If I come into your office asking you to help fix my broken left leg, please don't focus on helping my good arm or my good leg, instead," she said. Of course, it was easy for me to agree. LPA is a focused approach, after all.

There was one thing Joyce knew. She wasn't going to just stay home for the rest of her life. She also loved to drive (just not on bridges or in tunnels), and lived in the suburbs, so public transportation was out of the question. I was clearly dealing with a woman who was committed to overcoming her phobia but also completely in distress. Her work, economics, and also her personal dignity and self-respect were at stake. Being unable to overcome her phobia was depressing her so much, she said, that she felt like a failure, and she was afraid her weakness was going to start to show. As a lawyer, that would certainly diminish her ability to fight for her clients.

Joyce's Treatment

We started talking, just so I could get a picture of the nature of her fear. It was clear that her phobia happened only if she was alone and driving. If she was on a crowded bus, or a train, she was fine. She told me exactly how and what she felt, and I listened, and let her know that I believed her. That was especially important to her, she told me, given the way other therapists had insisted that when she explained how she felt, and what she wanted to do, she was trying to take control of the therapeutic situation. It is a common and unfortunate tactic in some forms of therapy to break down the patient's defenses and get at "the truth." But Joyce was telling me the truth. And as I told her, I was fine with her taking control if she wanted to. After all, she was trying to help herself, and in LPA, the patient has everything to do with the outcome.

I should also note that what I was doing as we spoke was lending not only my ear, but my support. And supportively listening to her also had the effect of slowing down her anxiety- driven frustration. As my father, the surgeon, used to say in his understated way, "You need to listen to the patient. You get a lot of information that way."

Joyce had already spent so much time with other therapists that she knew all about her phobia: over and over, she'd had to explain it, discuss it, but was never able to directly address it. I wasn't surprised: my experience with countless patients over the years is that they emerge from that kind of psychodynamic psychotherapy having learned a lot about themselves but still couldn't actually overcome the reason they were there in the first place.

In fact, in the first session, she was a little surprised at how quickly I shifted into philosophizing with her. She knew plenty about her phobia—she was quite an expert on it. So we began to talk about bridges, tunnels, and people in a much larger context. We got on the subject of inventions and engineering. Just acting on a hunch, I asked her who she thought had invented the wheel. She didn't know. Frankly, neither did I. So we tossed around some ideas: we agreed that the wheel was certainly invented by humans, and based on that, we began to embark on a philosophical discussion.

I began to encourage her to think philosophically about that idea of *The Family of Man*, a classic book and photo exhibit from many years ago that expressed the idea that we are all part of the same species. We're all related. We all share a wonderful capacity to create and invent. In essence, we are all part of that wheel.

"Interesting," I remember Joyce saying in a positive tone of voice. Clearly, she was struck by the idea.

I expanded that concept into the idea that since humanity created bridges and tunnels, and we are all part of this family of humanity, that meant that Joyce, too, was part of the creation of such structures. She began to talk about the efforts it must have taken to conceive of and create these. It was not a big leap to realize that she was connected to them, and then realize that by driving on these structures, these human-made inventions, she was in essence expressing and celebrating that connection. And she began to see herself as part of the construction and invention of these bridges and tunnels. By driving on them, or through them, she was in essence honoring the accomplishment of their being built.

No, it's not entirely logical. It's almost illogical. But it's this type of almost illogic that can be developed into a simple logic in order to define, in a narrow window, a new way of thinking that can begin to challenge and overcome the problem. And the nature of this illogical logic, in a sense, was not lost on Joyce at all. She actually liked the idea of being indirectly involved in the building of all of these remarkable structures. She liked the discussions and said they were truly slowing down her anxiety-ridden, phobic thinking. She liked having another way to consider things.

She found thinking about herself in this way new, different, and refreshing. And it was a relief to imagine herself, after all this time, in this new and brighter light. From this new vantage point, she could think about different ways for coping with her phobia. I was pretty clear we were getting to her phobia as we proceeded to challenge her thinking and she was all right with this. In other words, I let her know we were heading there, and she was comfortable enough to begin that part of the journey.

On the second visit, with this new perspective in place, we started the action phase to resolve (and disarm) Joyce's phobic response. I started by teaching Joyce a simple relaxation technique: sitting comfortably in an easy chair, she took a few deep breaths, and let herself float into a state of relaxation. We practiced this technique over and over until Joyce became an expert. Then we started working on a specific technique to desensitize Joyce to her phobic response. Since we were neither outside nor in a car, I had Joyce create all of this in her head. That's the beauty of LPA: you can do it anywhere, because all you need is your own imagination and a strategy.

Still in her relaxed state, I asked Joyce to imagine a big screen, like a movie screen, and then split it with a line down the middle. We just worked with the left side of that screen. I asked her to project some simple images of what she does well before she is actually near a bridge or a tunnel. I asked her to start by projecting images of the night before, and then images from breakfast, and then images from when she's just getting into her car and beginning her trip to work.

The images from the evening before were far less intense than those from breakfast the next morning or the start of her drive. And their progression, from less stressful to more stressful images, is part of the process. First, Joyce would project the easiest images, and then move forward, until she was actually able to visualize the actual drive over a bridge or through a tunnel. At first, imagining the process of getting into the car and starting it up immediately made her anxious. But I reminded her that she was just imagining this: it wasn't actually happening at all. It was just a visualization. Nothing could go wrong.

Then I added the next step. I asked Joyce to shift her focus over to the right side of the screen, which was still blank. I had her start by projecting some pleasant images on that side—being on vacation, imagining a great place she'd gone to. She projected the image of her honeymoon on a tropical island. These situations often make a patient feel more relaxed. And that's the beginning of the method at work, because as you practice, maybe five or six times a day and gain experience, soon you'll be able to easily switch sides of the screen: you'll be able to shift from the anxiety-provoking left side of the screen to the relaxing right side. It's that simple: shift from fear-inducing to calm-inducing. As you continue the process, the phobic response is decreased and even extinguished: eventually, most unpleasant images are incompatible with the pleasant, non-anxiety provoking images. The end result is that as you practice over and over with the imagery, it will have a positive effect on the real experience as the phobia is overcome.

In the next two sessions (the third and fourth) Joyce and I renewed our discussion of the tools humanity has made to make life easier, the innovations and constructions—and how Joyce herself was therefore connected to this tradition of invention and resourcefulness. She was captivated by this idea, and it gave her a great deal of security. She found herself more interested in thinking about how things were built than in focusing on her own fear. Given the right information and a format (the split screen) to work with, her brain was changing the channel for itself.

The entire process took four visits. I advised Joyce to keep practicing the split-screen technique. The plan was to follow up by phone in a month's time. This split-screen method gave Joyce a way to cope with the daily challenge of heading over a bridge or through a tunnel. By practicing all the time, she was able to become mentally desensitized to the phobia. When the time came to actually drive over a bridge, or through a tunnel, she could remember this coping method. In her mind, she had done it countless times. And since she wanted to cross the bridge, she wanted to go through the tunnel—because most of all, she wanted to get where she had to go, she was able to conquer her phobia. The will was supported by the method she practiced. She became desensitized. When she was driving, she could keep her mind on the pleasant imagery she'd created earlier—imagine herself on vacation or listening to gorgeous music, as so many of us do, when listening to the radio as many of us do, as she was crossing a bridge or heading through a tunnel. It made the journey far easier.

Safely to the Other Side

When we talked on the phone a month later, Joyce told me how well she was doing. She'd loved starting from the concept that we are all connected to the genius of human invention and creativity, and she had always been motivated to practice and conquer her phobia. The first few times she was headed for a bridge, she told me, she did feel stress and anxiety. But she reminded herself that it was only one side of the screen. And she kept practicing the strategy, of course not while driving. Before long, she was experiencing a sense of her own success: she could cross a bridge, even numerous times in one day. When she got to the other side, she said, she didn't experience a jittery sigh of relief, but a deeper sense of accomplishment. And a year later, she followed up with me again. "It's Joyce," she said on the phone in her bright and capable voice. "And I just wanted you to know I'm driving over bridges and through tunnels without having to use any strategies at all now." Instead of reinforcing the phobia, Joyce was reinforcing her success.

Were there any hitches? I wanted to know. She admitted that on occasion, if she was stuck sitting in heavy, stalled traffic, she might get a bit uncomfortable. But the feeling of unease didn't stop her, she said. She drove everywhere, regularly, and she got wherever she needed to go. I know she practiced, a lot, and she really worked at this—and that's such an essential part of the LPA process. You get out of it what you put into it, and if you practice as much as Joyce did, that's a lot.

Phobia Case Study #2: Mike Overcomes His Fear of Dogs

It's easy to tackle specific phobias, such as fear of bridges or dogs, when the **Action** sequence of LPA treatment includes measured, careful exposure to the source of the problem. Let me give you another example of exactly how that works.

I established a reputation early on for short-term treatments that helped patients make significant behavioral changes—sometimes in just one or two visits. A patient of mine who had needed just a single visit to help him quit smoking urged his friend Mike to come in and discuss a problem that was already bad and about to get worse. Mike needed help, and he didn't have much time to get it.

The problem had started back when Mike was a boy. He had simply never felt comfortable with dogs. It didn't matter if they were old or young, big or small, male or female, Poodle or Collie or German Shepherd or Pit Bull or a little Lhasa Apso: Mike just felt uneasy *whenever* there was a dog around. Over time, uneasiness turned into fear. During the past few years, he told me, the fear had become a phobia. And he lived in a high-rise apartment building. If a dog and his owner were in the elevator, he'd have to wait for the next car. Worse, when he saw someone coming toward him with a dog on a leash, he'd compulsively head across the street.

The mere thought of a dog had grown from a serious inconvenience to the dominating factor in his life. And now, as is often the case with phobias, matters were coming to a head. Which is when he came to me.

Having reconnected with an old friend from college who he hadn't seen in years, Mike had planned a visit in the upcoming spring to the city where his friend lived. But at some point, after they had started making plans for a reunion, when Mike had already bought his plane ticket, his friend got a dog. It had come out in a phone conversation, casually, as they recounted the latest news in each of their families. And this was an old dog, gentle and kind and benign.

Didn't matter. Suddenly the prospect of visiting his friend, despite everything else, was terrifying. Mike hit a wall. No matter how badly he wanted to see his friend, he was filled with dread at the idea of spending his visit around a dog. And he was in a total panic.

Mike's Treatment

When Mike arrived for his appointment, he started the session by asking if he should cancel his plans. Then he wondered if it was likely—or possible at all—that he could overcome his fear, even just enough to make the trip. And if he did get a handle on his phobia, there was no guarantee that it wouldn't suddenly flare up in the middle of his visit. There was a potential for any number of disasters if the worst did happen.

I reassured him that while some phobias required more time and effort than others, fears involving animals were easy to tackle and very treatable. So treatable, in fact, I can do my share of the work in just a session or two and let the patient take over from there.

I told Mike that if a person has a fear of, say, elevators or flying, factors such as claustrophobia, anxiety, and panic attacks are usually present to complicate the treatment and make the desensitization process a little harder. But with animals, patients very often have a clear idea of how the fear originated and, in my experience, just as often have a specific motivation to eliminate the phobia from their lives.

Mike had the motivation he needed to tackle his issue head on: he badly wanted to visit his friend. And, as he sat answering some of my questions about his past, the root of the phobia became more and more apparent. I got Mike to talk about the first time he remembered associating dogs with scary thoughts. Realizing your first time experiencing phobic thoughts can really tell you a lot.

Mike thought for a moment and then told me that he had an early memory of hearing his mother and grandmother talk about dogs. He was very young and had no previous contact whatsoever with dogs. He overheard one of them say that dogs could hurt people and dog bites could cause rabies. To someone so young, with no dog experience, this was terrifying. And to make matters worse, it was a subject they talked about quite often.

Hearing something once is one thing, but hearing it over and over had essentially taught him there was every reason to be terrified of dogs. So, of course, he developed a fear of them.

Patients often have theories they share with their doctors about what is causing their back pain or how they reactivated an old knee injury, and the same thing holds true in psychiatry. I simply accepted Mike's theory. I did not question the validity of what he said. I didn't try to take control of the situation and analyze it. I believed him. For one thing, there's no point in not believing him. For another, the work I am doing with these kinds of phobias is to effect a behavioral change that ultimately, by using LPA, lets a patient change his entire way of thinking about a problem. The goal is as rapid but effective a resolution as possible. Far too many traditional therapists would have focused on what sort of thoughts came up while revisiting the conversations between his mother and grandmother, and how those thoughts made him feel. This usually leads people far, far off course, and away from directly addressing their phobia.

Mike and I moved onto the next phase of LPA: philosophizing. We spent a little time examining the nature of what his mother and grandmother used to say. Did he think their fears might have been a little overblown? I asked. He thought about it, and decided that yes, they were, adding that they had a lot of anxieties about death and danger in general. Again, the emphasis was on his thinking rather than an open-ended exploration of his feelings. From there, we discussed the concept of "possibilities vs. probabilities," or what was likely versus what wasn't. So, it's *possible* that a dog might bite Mike, and it's also *possible* he might get rabies, but what are the *probabilities*?

After a little reflection, Mike concluded that the probability of anything bad happening was slim to nearly none. Mike brought up a number of different scenarios that provoked his phobic response and we went through each one gauging the possible versus the probable. Mike eventually found himself laughing at how outlandish some of those possibilities were. Looking at situations with that criteria is one of the exercises you can do by yourself in this book, and I've created a chart to start you out. We'll get to that.

Finally, we moved onto phase three of LPA: action. In this case, action meant behavior modification. One way of desensitizing Mike was by setting up short, safe periods of time when he had exposure to a dog. The idea behind desensitization is that through repeated but safe exposure, you gradually unlearn your fear. I encouraged him to buy a book about dog breeds that described their different traits, training needs, behavior, and personalities. He chose a great one: *The Complete Dog Book* by the American Kennel Club. For a week, he pored through it every night, reading about the different breeds and studying the photos and then reported his reactions back to me. Interestingly, he was not uncomfortable with the book and its pictures, and actually enjoyed the learning experience.

Then came his real-life exposure to a dog. To achieve this, he reached out to a dog-owning friend who was completely trustworthy, as was her gentle and even-tempered dog. Trustworthiness in the dog owner is critical, as you'll see. They set up meetings for a half an hour every day over the course of a week. At each meeting, Mike would stand a distance away from his friend and her dog. His friend sat very still, always in the same place, holding her gentle dog on a leash. Each day, Mike moved a little closer, a few feet at a time. They had arranged beforehand that she would *never* move toward Mike with her dog.

After about a week, Mike realized that he was capable of putting the final step of the plan into action. He had finally gotten near enough, and he was calm enough, to reach out and gently pet the dog. The dog was happy to receive the affection, and Mike realized that the fear that had plagued him for so much of his life had disappeared, replaced by a new sense of joy. He began petting his friend's dog for longer and longer periods of time. Mike had overcome his phobia.

A Matter of Trust

It's a key part of this strategy that the person conquering the phobia is in complete control of the situation. Mike trusted his friend to keep her dog leashed and close by her side, and knew he could approach at his own pace. His trust assured him nothing unexpected could happen. Maybe it was *possible*, but he knew for certain it wasn't *probable*.

Mike had only needed a single two-hour session to discuss the issue. I was able to offer him an action-based strategy to solve the problem and, if he wanted, the option of returning for another visit to work with split-screen visualization.

When something is done in the lab, not in real life, the medical term for it is in vitro. Because Mike had such strong drive to make the treatment work, which in turn made him more than capable of doing so, we decided to use an *in vivo*—or, real life—approach. The action-oriented strategy meant he did most of the work by himself. This was, in fact, one of the sessions that inspired me to further develop LPA and give patients a set of strategies—just like a diet or exercise regimen—allowing them to conquer their fears powered by their own motivation to succeed.

Phobia Case Study #3: The Stage Fright Quartet

LPA is an extremely effective strategy for conquering the crippling social phobia loosely known as stage fright. The truth is, you don't have to be anywhere near a stage to feel stage fright. You might be a parent facing a PTA meeting, a teacher in front of a classroom, or a corporate professional doing a presentation for a meeting. It's the same basic terror, regardless of its form.

Like other phobias, stage fright can originate in endlessly different ways, and no two versions will be exactly the same. But I've treated dancers, singers, musicians, actors, and non-performers as well for whom the prospect of having to appear in public triggered extreme, uncontrollable anxiety. Imagining having to perform or speak in public is so stressful in itself that the person would rather do *anything* else. We all have instances where we shy away from something we don't want to do, for a variety of reasons, and if we can make an excuse to drop out, some of us do. But in the case of people who make their living performing, excuses can be tremendously dangerous—nearly as dangerous as the phobia itself. On the one hand, they're at risk of having to change careers, and on the other hand, they can't bear what they have to do. In all the performers I've treated, I have to say that I never met one who wasn't riddled with anxiety. It's a tough job.

Working with socially phobic patients, I have been able to push beyond the phobic response with them, and they have continued in their careers and gone on to perform magnificently, or speak in public brilliantly. In the framework and discipline of LPA, we review *how* the phobia developed, take a philosophical look at *why* it developed, and then we proceed to an action-based strategy to overcome it. Patients learn how to put themselves in a relaxed state—a tool they can use to fight those dreadful feelings of fear and paralysis anytime they need to, and learn how to replace those feelings with other, positive feelings. What happens is that a patient learns how to desensitize himself or herself without denying anything about the phobia. He or she just moves past it.

Variations on a Theme

Instead of a single example of someone who came to me to overcome stage fright, I'm going to talk about a whole group of them. What's interesting is that in all of their cases, they were at tremendous risk because of this phobia. All were people in show business: dancers and musicians (one a piano player, one a singer), so stage fright, unmanaged, could be a career death sentence. For each, a paralysis had set in, caused by their own irrational anxiety and fear, that threatened to prevent them from doing what they *had* to do to earn their living: perform on stage. If they didn't overcome their stage fright, not only would they be out of a job, but all of those years of study, all those thousands of hours of practice and dedication would be for nothing. The pressure was tremendous on all of them.

Also, all tried to work through it. None of these people were the type to give up. They had learned to be tenacious to sustain their careers, to practice, to stay fit, and land gigs, and so they forced themselves to perform, anyway. Sometimes the anxiety would go away. But at other times it didn't—and then, it was hellish to perform.

As is often the case with phobias, when a patient's phobic response leads to anxious states and possible avoidant behavior, clear thinking is hampered. Before they reached out to me, each of these patients had already become so anxious and fearful that going onstage was already entirely problematic. Sometimes, they went onstage and made mistakes they'd otherwise never make. Or they were just not able to give it their all, and therefore did not get that great energy back from the audience that makes it all worthwhile. Or they wound up having to desperately concoct alibis, creating sham excuses as to why they couldn't go to work that night and felt terrible about that. They came to me because they *had* to do something about their fears—and soon— or they'd lose their very livelihood.

In all cases—and this is important from the point of view of a psychiatrist — none of these patients had additional, compounding issues. None had any of the markers that would indicate a far deeper underlying problem, such as depression, or a specific or generalized anxiety disorder. None had substance issues that would affect their behavior. And though they all shared the same irrational, overwhelming fear of getting onstage to perform, in each case the phobia had a different origin.

The Dancer Who Fell and the Singer Who Got Sick: Phobias with a Direct Cause

In these first two cases, something very specific happened to each performer, and it's no mystery that they would develop a phobia. The cause was direct and clear. In each case, each person suffered a glitch in their own program that had potentially disastrous consequences, and a whole range of unpleasant experiences tagged along with it. But we knew the *why*—in fact, *they* knew it even before I asked them. And I knew I could help them. Such phobias—a direct result of a particular event—are, in my experience, extremely straightforward to address. First, let's look at the problem each performer had.

The dancer who was afraid to fall had already fallen. That was the problem. When she came into my office, she was already an up and coming Broadway dancer, and her dancing career was just starting to take off. Usually when she danced, she was sure of herself, moving confidently and beautifully all around the stage. And then, one single performance proved her undoing.

On stage, in previews, in front of a full audience and in the middle of her performance, she leapt into the air as she normally did: same dance, same leap. But this time, as she landed on the stage, something happened. Maybe she was distracted momentarily. Maybe she had just had a subtle but devastating loss of balance. Maybe she slipped. As she recounted the fall to me, those details were fuzzy. "I don't remember it all," she said. But what was crystal clear in her mind was that when she fell, she could feel every eye in the audience upon her. The entire theater watched her lose her balance.

She was mortified, as any of us would be. But it wasn't just a bad moment. Instead of getting over it, it got hold of her. Days later, the fall kept replaying itself in her head. She was still in rehearsals; nevertheless, she had to get back onstage to perform. But the prospect of getting back on that stage was nerve-wracking. Every time she imagined herself performing again, she had visions of taking another fall and imagined all those faces—looking at her.

Her anxiety around this became so severe that she developed serious, crippling stage fright. She simply could not and would not get back up on that stage, she told me. But she was a professional dancer, at the beginning point in her career. The work we had to do wasn't going to be a long, drawn-out "Do you remember the first time you got onstage as a child" kind of approach. She had to be able to get back on stage and *fast*, or her life as she knew it would be over.

Then there was the singer who was terrified of getting sick on stage and had already gotten sick on stage. That's why she was in my office. She was a successful singer-songwriter with lots of fans and drew large audiences wherever she performed. One night during a show, she began feeling sick. She got queasy; her stomach began to rumble. She tried to just play and sing right through her nausea, but it got worse and worse. There she was, under the lights, when finally, the worst happened: she threw up in front of the entire club, right there on stage.

Of course, it's not unusual for even the most experienced entertainers to feel jittery about a performance. And no one enjoys being sick, whether it's in private or—especially— in a very public place. But the magnitude of what happened to her, with all of its sense of shame and its implications, just kept growing. It quickly morphed from just a very unfortunate but isolated night to something amorphous and terrifying. It seized her very concept of performance and turned it inside out. Instead of seeing performing as an opportunity to express herself, she now imagined it as an inevitable, awful humiliation. And though the singer was not sick and had no signs that she would get sick again, she was convinced the odds of her repeating that awful night were high. She became obsessed with the possibility.

So she carried on. But the longer she lived with her phobia, the more it affected her performances. When you can't put your heart and soul into a performance, your audience knows it—especially in the intimate setting of a nightclub. If she didn't find a way to overcome this, she knew that soon she would begin to lose her audience, and then her bookings would dwindle, and there would go her career.

For both these people, the phases of LPA that we spent the most time on would be the learning phase and the action phase. Why? They already knew why they had a phobia, they learned it from the specific events that led to it, and they knew it was crippling their careers and their lies. We didn't need to spend much time philosophizing, which would extend us into a vast number of issues about their lives. In this case, due to the clarity of the event that befell these people, the cause was clear.

The Shadow Dancer and the Rock Star: Phobias with Deeper Roots

Now let's shift gears to two other performers. In their cases, their phobias were not quite as simple. From my perspective as a psychiatrist, the difference was that there was also an older cause that compounded the phobia, a layer or earlier trigger that had to be understood and connected to what they were now trying so hard to avoid. Even though we were not going to embark on years of psychoanalysis or psychodynamic therapy, unpacking every facet of their past and attempt to unlock countless doors to their unconscious and subconscious, we had some additional work to do. Despite that, both were phobic individuals who did the best they could to charge right through their own phobic response. By sheer force of will, they overcame their anxiety with a firm "I must do this" approach. But they still suffered, terribly. So it was important to ease that underlying pain.

Certainly, it's common for performers—especially dancers—to be self-conscious about their weight. They have to be conscious of everything about their bodies—it's not just a question of looks. But in the case a professional dancer who came to see me, his appearance had become a vexing obsession. He was terrified—not of *being* overweight, but of being *perceived* as overweight—actually, of having his *shadow* seen as overweight in a particular performance.

The distinction is important, because it would play a role in how we worked through his phobia. He was a highly disciplined professional dancer who had been at it for years, put in years of physically demanding work in the studio and on stage, and he was strong and fit. When we talked, he explained that while he was happy if someone described him as thin, he hadn't obsessed much about his weight outside of the context of performing. "All dancers worry about their appearance," he said. "It's part of the job."

He knew that being overweight could have a seriously negative impact on his career—but looking overweight could as well. He was getting older: that natural willowy shape of youth was a little different now. Aging in itself was a liability: most dancers hit their peak of ability when they're pretty young. But even then, he wasn't that worried.

So what happened? He was dancing in a performance that required him to dance behind a scrim, a layered, translucent curtain that created a shadow dancer, and the shadow itself wasn't as well defined or as etched as he was. The audience would be watching his shadow, and he knew, from watching other dancers behind that scrim, that it made all of them look larger. The choreographer, who was watching from the audience, made a remark that some of the dancers looked, to be blunt, fat. It was a result of the layers, an illusion. But he was one of the dancers onstage at the time. And it took him back to some old memories from when he was a young boy, growing up in a family where being thin was always important, and fat people were criticized. And that's where the phobia began to creep up on him.

My point here is that we did address memories. But we did it as part of LPA. LPA isn't just a step-by-step approach that never goes in depth. It does. In this case, that was a vital part of working to overcome the phobia. Having grown up in a family that was obsessed with being thin, he was entirely unprepared for being called fat, even inadvertently. That's all it took. In his mind, all the audience would see when he danced in this work was his shadow, and how grossly overweight it appeared—and then they would see *him* as fat. It didn't take long before concern and anxiety turned into a fear so acute that he couldn't bear the idea of performing in public.

And then there was the piano player. He was part of an extremely well-known and successful rock band. And he was a wreck. When he came in for a consultation, he sat down—this very rock 'n' roll-looking man in flamboyant clothes—and with a kind of shudder, recounted how, a few months before, he had showed up late for a show. He did it one night, and then he did it the next night.

He sat in my office in his custom snakeskin boots, head in his hands. His lateness didn't go unnoticed, he told me. His boss—the bandleader—took him aside and said, essentially, "Get it together. Shape up. Start focusing. Do your job."

Although he'd been late, the first time, just for some logistical reason, it had started to work on him. And as he'd go on to tell me, as a kid he was a daydreamer. He had a sensitive, artistic personality. And his parents, no-nonsense types, had made it clear they thought he'd amount to nothing, not a good thing to hear growing up. So now combine that memory with this new situation where his boss was telling him he was messing up. It triggered a fear that he really would amount to nothing, that he had no business being on stage—even though he was an amazingly gifted piano player, with tons of style and charisma. The whole package. He had learned, growing up, to not believe in himself. And how he processed being scolded by his boss as proof. But again, this was learned—it wasn't deeply buried. It was all there, under the surface, and he understood it.

Instead of taking the advice of his bandleader, he set himself on a downward spiral. He wasn't late, but he became obsessed with not being able to play well. He began forgetting certain changes, making tiny little mistakes, missing a chorus, a bridge, forgetting what song they were playing—but he was so skilled that he covered all of this up. But he knew it was happening. He became incredibly self-conscious on stage, fearful of his own fingers, and that, of course, caused him to make more mistakes. This was a disaster; a self-fulfilling nightmare. The worse he felt, the worse he played—and what he was doing was proving to himself that he wasn't up to it. Now he was terrified he was going to make more mistakes, make the band look bad, and ultimately, lose the gig.

When I asked him what else had happened besides his boss talking to him—which is certainly not unheard of; that's a bandleader's job—it came to light that he had broken up with his girlfriend some time before he'd gotten a talking-to about his playing. That, in his mind, was another failure, even though there were perfectly good reasons why they broke up that had more to do with their incompatible lifestyles than his being any kind of failure. But we now had another failure as he saw it. And the anxiety he felt before a performance was almost unbearable. So we had to get him over it.

A Similar Treatment Works for All by Emphasizing Different Aspects of the LPA.

I was able to help all of these performers using LPA. First of all, I agreed they all had a reason to be anxious—and again, affirming that was a positive first step. Instead of denying each patient's fears as ungrounded, I empathized. After all, you can't fall or develop an imagined or real weight problem when you're a professional dancer. You can't get sick in the middle of a singing, or forget the song you're supposed to be playing, when you're a working musician.

Had these patients tried addressing their phobias with the standard talk therapy approach, they might still be in their therapist's office today, and no nearer to a real resolution of the problem that drove them to seek help in the first place. Frankly, none of these patients could afford to spend years exploring the complexities of their lives as individuals or performers. They had commitments and responsibilities—and they needed a solution quickly.

A psychiatric nurse practitioner friend of mine once said that using traditional methods of talk therapy for these sorts of issues was like tearing down a house plus taking the rest of the town with it, clearly a pretty drastic approach to treating a phobia. So we set about fixing the issues.

The falling dancer and the sick singer knew the *why*, so we worked most on the learning and the action phases. The shadow dancer and the rock pianist had phobias that grew out of something more deeply buried. Their anxieties stemmed from some belief or idea about themselves and how they would be seen by others, not from a specific incident. The dancer was afraid to be seen as fat, and the pianist was afraid to be seen as a fraud.

With these sorts of clients, I tend to focus more attention on the philosophizing phase of LPA, as they need to understand how their anxieties are rooted in moments from their past. That's how we got to the shadow dancer's family. He told me that all his family members were thin and proud of it. He'd had a neighbor who could be generously described as "full-figured," and his parents were extremely critical of the way that neighbor looked—and made it clear to their son, then a young dancer. It was what you might call an "aha" moment. He stopped what he was saying, sat back, and said, "Wait a minute—now I get it."

And I said, "You're absolutely right."

The piano player had also had a very formative experience when he was younger. After telling me about his recent break-up, we got to talking about how he grew up. He told me that as a boy, he was prone to daydreaming. In school, three different teachers had criticized him for his inability to concentrate, and had told his parents, who were understandably vexed. One teacher even suggested he "would never get very far in life." That a teacher would say that to an impressionable child, and his parents would repeat it, really underscores the influence figures like teachers, let alone parents, can have in our lives. One comment, made out of frustration or snap judgment, can stick with us for years to come. Discussing those incidents was the sort of philosophizing we needed to do in order to understand how learned experiences are extrapolated into overwhelming phobic responses.

Because as children, we believe what we're told, whether it's true or not. And it can have a profound influence on us and our self-esteem for the rest of our lives.

Action: The Split Screen

Once I've worked with each patient to get through the learning and philosophizing phases, we are ready to concentrate on action. So now that we've seen how it works with the other examples, I'm going to go a bit more in depth about the technique that worked so well with Joyce's bridge phobia.

The **split screen technique** is a modified version of what's called a systematic desensitization program. The method was developed by Dr. Joseph Wolpe, a pioneer of behavioral based therapy. Essentially, it involves a step-by-step process in which a **hierarchy of anxieties**, from least to more intense, is gradually presented to the person.

I like to use a split movie screen to do this. I focus on projecting and seeing the **hierarchy of anxieties** on the left side of this movie screen, so the patient sees the anxiety, but does not experience it. This can be combined with *in vitro* (in your head) flooding, in which seeing the anxieties over and over leads to the anxieties being less and less intense until eventually, they don't bother the person at all.

In addition, I also like adding the process of **reciprocal inhibition**—where relaxation is taught, and is most often incompatible with the phobic anxiety. I use the blank right side of the screen for the person to visualize pleasant scenes or thoughts, i.e., the relaxing images of their choosing. This step reduces the stress from the phobic situation further and further from the phobic anxiety visualizations on the left side of the screen.

I have found that combining and modifying these three methods gives me the best results in the action phase of LPA. In terms of stage fright, performers usually have some unique abilities to use their imagination, so this type of imagery works very well to eliminate their phobias. It can work equally well for the person giving a PTA talk or presenting at a business meeting, though often, they need more practice with this new set of skills.

But before we get to the split screen, we practice relaxing. The first step is to help the patients relax and cool down the anxiety's overheated circuitry, so they can focus on some of the more nuanced details of their phobias.

First, the patient relaxes comfortably in a chair and takes a series of deep breaths, inhaling and exhaling over and over, with me guiding them into this relaxed state. It's very similar to something many people do on their own in yoga or meditation practices, or are guided through in mindfulness classes. Usually, in a few moments, the patient finds herself in a **restful state**, able to concentrate on specific thoughts.

After the patient comes out of the restful state, I engage him or her in a conversation about the problem, revisiting the learning and philosophizing aspects of the phobia. I instruct the patient to again reenter the relaxed state, this time doing it by herself or with at least a minimum of guidance. In this way, the patient learns the relaxation technique on her own and will be able to use it long after leaving the treatment setting.

Next, I ask the patient to visualize a large movie screen. I instruct her to project herself onto it, seeing herself calm and enjoying the best things in life. Then, I slowly bring her closer to the phobic situation, through images that move in a hierarchy from pleasant and stress-free to those that are directly involved with her anxiety. She observes the action onscreen and keeps enough of a distance to avoid experiencing the trauma associated with the accident.

If her emotions start running at a higher pitch, I tell her to cut away from the phobia imagery and replace it with something soothing and pleasant. Often, stressful images are entirely incompatible with pleasant images and the pleasant images "win out." This adds the **reciprocal inhibition** segment to the treatment program, combining a pleasant experience–visualization–with a phobic situation.

The patient repeatedly watches the phobic situation on the screen, with her anxiety rising and subsequently dissipating; this is called *in vitro flooding*. We have now combined three behavior modification techniques into one continuous action phase of the program. It's a triple-strategy therapy and, in my experience, leads to good results. I find this is particularly true for performers because of their strength of imagination.

For those of us who aren't used to dancing, singing, or making music in front of an audience, getting into the relaxing state and using the three techniques may take more time — but not a lot more. Once you're there, however, and ready to put the LPA techniques to work, practicing is crucial—just as crucial as stretching before a race or studying for a test. Or running through scales, memorizing lyrics, and rehearsing dance steps over and over. This is one area where performers often have an advantage; they're in front of an audience because they've put so much work and effort into learning their craft. And it's one area the rest of us should emulate when we put LPA to work.

Practice and repetition also allow the patient to focus on the action phase treatment she finds most effective. Once the patient and I work through the process so he or she is able to repeat it eight–ten times with me in the room, she decides which technique — or combination of techniques — works best. I have the patient practice for a minute or two ten times a day, so when the time comes, she can make the anxiety dissipate, letting her get back to their place in front of an audience. And that's right where she belongs.

PART TWO

Anxiety

CHAPTER 7

When Worry and Anxiety Become Obsession

Anxiety is a pervasive condition in modern society. It's completely understandable for people to be anxious about actual problems, both personal and societal, and imagined ones—those endless *what-if* questions that can keep us up at night. And anxiety even has its charms. We're all familiar with the archetype of the anxious New Yorker in countless Woody Allen movies, someone who can never stop worrying even when there is nothing, really to worry about. But for millions of Americans, anxiety is no laughing matter. It's an epidemic in this country. Generalized Anxiety Disorder—GAD—affects some 5 percent of the entire U.S. population. But the real rate of Generalized Anxiety Disorder may be even higher. At any given time, anxiety disorder clinics report that 25 percent of their patients in these programs suffer from GAD (*Synopsis of Psychiatry,* Benjamin Sadock and Virginia A. Sadock, (Philadelphia: Lippincott, Williams & Wilkins, 2002]).

And that's just the people whose level of general anxiety rates a clinical diagnosis. From my perspective, I prefer to view anxiety disorders as a whole spectrum set of disorders that include subthreshold and subclinical forms, much like PTSD (post-traumatic stress disorder).

As is the case with the so-called bible of our field, the *DSM*, Generalized Anxiety Disorder has been defined and redefined many times. I'm including the definition here because even the language of that definition itself is a cause for anxiety, at least to me as a psychiatrist:

> The presence of excessive anxiety and worry about a variety of topics, events, or activities. Worry occurs more often than not for at least 6 months and is clearly excessive.

As I said, there's plenty in the way of legitimate concerns to worry about. If we use a more broad-based definition, many more people suffer from some form of GAD than are officially documented. People suffering may have impaired concentration, extreme restlessness, excessive muscle tension, headaches, sleep disturbances, autonomic hyperactivity (physical symptoms of anxiety, such as shortness of breath, dizziness, sweating, racing heartbeat), obsessive behaviors and thoughts. Other symptoms will make it difficult just to get through a given day. Anxiety patients may be consumed by irrational fears, endless, unstoppable what-ifs, and be trapped in a ping-pong game of all-or-nothing thinking that makes even the simplest decision impossible.

CHAPTER **8**

Treating Anxiety

The Trouble with Medications

What happens when people finally turn to a therapist for help? All too often, they get the wrong kind of treatment. Generations of stressed-out Americans have been prescribed anti-anxiety medications, most often, the benzodiazapines, or the "benzos. As mentioned earlier, the first one to be sold commercially was Librium, in 1960. A few years later came Valium, followed by the more recent, and now most popular variations: Ativan, Klonopin, and Xanax, as noted earlier. All are listed as controlled substances, as they are highly addicting, with a number of withdrawal issues. They're also dangerous when combined with certain pain medications, such as opiates. So while these drugs certainly can be helpful in many circumstances, they require rigorous monitoring, and many clinicians are moving away from them.

Again, another group of medications being used are SSRIs, (selective serotonin reuptake inhibitors), which were originally used to treat depression. In 1987 Prozac was introduced, followed by Zoloft, Paxil, Celexa, and Lexapro. All are now used and approved for treating anxiety. While they don't have the same dangers (and are not listed as controlled substances), some therapists and patients report that they're not as effective for treating anxiety as the benzodiazepines.

From my standpoint, I have issues with prescribing a pill to cure certain anxiety problems. Certainly, many pharmaceutical products are truly lifesaving and are successful at treating many mental and physical disorders. But for anxiety there are other options that do not require a pill. Whether it's Cognitive Behavior Therapy (CBT), guided imagery and the LPA, these approaches offer successful alternatives that are long lasting without a pill. These methods give the patients tools to draw on whenever they need to, and there are no side effects or the risk of diminished concentration or memory. The American College of Physicians even recommended CBT as first line treatment for insomnia recently. Ironically, it's been found that anti-anxiety medications can have an adverse effect on sleep patterns.

Too Anxious to Talk

The other common referral for anxiety disorders is lengthy talk therapies such as traditional psychodynamic therapy or daily psycho-analysis, which may take years. Though they can be effective, these slower-paced therapies are aimed at uncovering the deep roots of anxiety issues, when all the patient really wants is to treat the anxiety that's consuming his life in the "here and now."

Open-ended questions, like the classic, "How does that make you feel?" or "What memories come to mind?" can cause anxiety in and of themselves. Why? They're exploratory, generalized questions that are open to interpretation—and yes, they may *eventually* tap the root of the problem. But in the meantime, there's still an anxious person suffering.

Treating Anxiety with LPA

The Learning, Philosophizing, and Action (LPA) approach I take with patients aims at identifying and solving the immediate problem fast. We work to challenge faulty beliefs, and create a new way to think about the problem in a short time, using effective relaxation techniques and breathing exercises, guided imagery, and other tools. And the interesting part of this approach is that for the most part, it works.

In contrast to the complications of taking anti-anxiety medication, there's something very calming about the fact that you *can* calm down. I treated a patient who was suffering from the anxiety of taking anti-anxiety medication. He was a business executive, a serious, competent, smart guy. His doctor had prescribed a benzodiazepine to treat his recurring anxiety. Which, ironically enough, added an element of yet more anxiety to his existing anxiety condition: the executive was terrified of becoming what he called a "benzo addict."

That's when the patient was referred to me. I taught him straightforward relaxation exercises, and challenged his worrisome negative and often inaccurate thoughts by getting him to reframe the issues. With this two-pronged approach, I was able to help him. He was relieved that no drugs were involved, and that relief motivated him to do what it took to feel better.

CHAPTER 9

Overcoming Anxiety With LPA: Real Stories

The examples that follow include a quartet of people with confirmed GAD, and subthreshold and subclinical variants on the anxiety spectrum. As is so often the case, they were affected both mentally and physically. Though successful professionals living productive lives, inside they were nervous wrecks. You'll meet a patient with GAD who became obsessed with media coverage of a flu epidemic; a pregnant woman whose situation-based anxiety centered on financial issues and maternity leave; a dentist with a combined diagnosis of anxiety, depression, and Obsessive-Compulsive Personality Disorder (OCPD); and a physics professor who was anxiety-ridden due to an obsessive vision of being swarmed by locusts. In all cases, LPA proved effective. Not only did these patients safely address the anxieties that brought them into my office, they were given a toolkit for rethinking strategies and calming down that each person could practice and draw on for the rest of their lives.

Anxiety Case Study #1: Dan: Stricken with a Terror of Illness

Anxiety can be triggered by a lot of different events. Some years ago, at the height of New York City's H1N1 "swine flu" scare, I treated a man who suffered from such severe anxiety about getting sick that he could barely get through the day.

Dan was in his late thirties, an insurance broker who lived in a prosperous suburb just outside the city. He was healthy and looked pretty fit, but he was overwhelmed by reports about the terrible flu epidemic the media was predicting and obsessed by the notion that he would get sick. He'd asked his primary care doctor for medication to help him calm down, but the doctor reminded him that this wasn't a new situation. Although in the past the doctor had prescribed anti-anxiety medications for Dan, he felt it was time for Dan to see a specialist who could treat his anxiety directly. That's when Dan was referred to me.

This wasn't the first time Dan had sought help from a psychotherapist. During our first visit, he told me that when he was in college, he had seen a campus therapist for help with his extreme anxiety over schoolwork and grades. He also told me that although he had always worried excessively about getting sick, news reports about this predicted flu were overwhelming him to the point where he was not only anxious, but terrified. "I can't sleep at all," he told me.

I looked at him. He was hunched forward in his chair, his eyes darting around and foot tapping. He was a nervous wreck, his whole body twisted with tension. Even his voice sounded breathy, as if he was gasping for air. Of course, he couldn't sleep.

Dan went on to tell me how anxious he always became as winter approached, since it was the season that brought colds and flu. In fact, any mention of an impending flu season or epidemic would set him off. He couldn't stop worrying and obsessing over every piece of flu-related news he read or saw on TV. He told me he became an obsessive researcher, collecting any information he could on every flu outbreak—where it hit, how fast it was spreading, how severe the symptoms were, the number of cases in New York City. After hearing of a flu death or serious complications, his mind would start racing, and he would end up with a headache and a serious case of indigestion and, often, to be honest, the runs. Food raced through him. He made sure to follow any precautions he could to make sure that he did not get sick, washing his hands again and again, especially after he had to shake somebody's hand. All this would dominate a major part of his day.

A Constant State of Worry

The medical term for Dan's symptoms is autonomic hyperactivity, which can include shortness of breath, accelerated heartbeat, shaking, sweating, dry mouth, dizziness, upset stomach, and so on. That, along with his constant worrying and his "cognitive vigilance"—or obsession with gathering information about the flu —were consistent with a Generalized Anxiety Disorder. Dan, like so many suffering from GAD, was mentally and physically hamstrung, and profoundly susceptible to alarmist, official, and media-generated messages. And yet, in a sense, who could blame him? The news reports were filled at that time with talk of outbreaks, epidemics, and the "pandemic" transmission of swine flu and other hot-button diseases. (Ebola and Zika virus are more recent examples of this kind of coverage.) Some of the media coverage was accurate. But some was so extremely overhyped that it could trigger a profound panic attack even in someone who isn't suffering from anxiety. The frightening remarks Dan heard in this daily media barrage resembled a group cognitive therapy session gone wrong, where common-sense thinking was challenged with doom and gloom perspectives that stimulate even more anxiety, as opposed to challenging anxiety with more perspective and a rational approach.

Media reports on serious public health issues like swine flu generally offer little in the way of reassurance or hope, instead laying the groundwork for increased anxiety and stress in the entire population. For people like Dan who suffer from generalized anxiety and a specific fear of becoming sick, media broadcasts that spread alarming information around the clock are a living nightmare.

At that period of time, however, even my concerns were raised: expert after expert made ominous comparisons of H1N1 flu to a disastrous influenza epidemic that had ravaged the country a century ago, when our medical knowledge was far less advanced than it is today. The term "pandemic" (which refers to the global spread of an illness, not its intensity) was used far too often without context or definition. It's a frightening-sounding word.

Whenever Dan read an article or listened to a news report about the seriousness of the upcoming flu season, it sent him into a state of terror. His GAD symptoms increased. And yet—also part of his disorder, as I mentioned—he was obsessed with hearing every detail of these reports. He *had* to listen. He was caught in a tremendously dangerous mental vise.

But there was one voice—one—during the media's coverage of H1N1 swine flu that offered clinical insights, reassurance, and balance. It belonged to Dr. Thomas R. Frieden, the New York City health commissioner (he was later appointed director of the Centers for Disease Control and Prevention by President Obama). In television interviews, Dr. Frieden, an infectious disease specialist, provided perspective that was measured and thoughtful. It offered a rational bright light that was much needed.

Helping Dan

That's exactly the kind of approach I used with Dan. Cognitive therapy is aimed at using rational thinking to challenge out-of-control thoughts and behaviors in order to alter and redefine those thoughts and behaviors. So providing an anxious patient with a wider range of options can provide some relief and offer new strategies. Like so many others, Dan just wanted to find freedom fast.

As we've already seen in the chapter on phobias, a person who is fearful of crossing bridges or going through tunnels can be offered various ways to rethink and restructure the thoughts and behavior surrounding her phobia. We spend time Learning about the problem, Philosophizing about its origins and how it's affecting the patient now, and then we start creating a plan of Action to overcome it. This step-by-step approach is extremely effective for treating Generalized Anxiety Disorders. Much like Dr. Frieden's approach, it allows the person to return to a calm state of mind, despite all the noise around them.

What's Possible Isn't Probable

Dan and I would work together for five months. I used the possible/probable approach with Dan, which proved very effective. First, I invited him to ponder the possibility that the world would end tomorrow. I asked, "Is it *possible*?"

"Yes," he said, twisting his hands.

Then I asked, "Is it *probable*"?

As a reaction to that question, Dan blinked. This fidgeting, toe-tapping, hunched over man sat up, furrowed his brow, and then blinked. Even the most anxious patient can see the difference immediately, and usually gets a good laugh at the unreality of the possibility, but not probability, of the world ending tomorrow. In Dan's case, I got a tentative smile out of him. "I get your point," he told me.

As my sessions with Dan continued, we created a series of challenges using possibilities versus probabilities to consider many of his GAD-related worries, including his rampant concerns about catching the flu. Is it possible? Sure. But is it probable? I asked Dan, "How many times have you actually had the flu?" Amazingly, he had never had the flu. Not once.

I asked him why not, and Dan told me he gets a flu shot every year, though he admitted that he always worried the shot itself would give him the flu. I asked if he was aware that the flu vaccine uses an attenuated (dead) virus, and that a dead virus can't spread an illness. We also discussed various medications that could ease the symptoms of flu if, in Dan's worst-case scenario, he did get sick.

At first this logical approach didn't seem to work for him. As a person obsessed with research, Dan liked logic. And he liked learning more about the vaccine and the flu. But it didn't help lessen his worry, fear, or anxiety. So I continued to ask him questions. In his workplace of thirty or so people, I asked him, how many had actually gotten the flu? Dan thought for a moment. He said "one or two" of his colleagues had recently been sick, but on further reflection, he realized they might just have had a cold. He also told me that his company brought in a nurse to give flu shots every year, and that employees were all encouraged to work from home if they were feeling ill, or just to stay home and recover. Talking about this, it suddenly dawned on Dan what a safe place he worked in. But before he could really explore that idea, he changed the subject in mid-sentence to his fears of catching the flu while on public transportation — or just from the air he breathed in the street. It was almost as if he couldn't, and wouldn't, allow himself to start feeling better.

So I asked why he'd shifted so quickly from thoughts of safety back to thoughts that made him fearful. He really had no answer. Instead, he anxiously repeated, "What about public transportation?" So, again using logic, I asked him how he got to work. Dan lived and worked in the suburbs, and drove the five miles to and from work in his own car. He didn't carpool. He certainly didn't take buses, trains, or subways to work.

It's not that he was trying to be manipulative here. GAD can really lead you into a whole trap of "what ifs," which is very common in anxiety-ridden people. "What if a bird flies into the engine?" for the anxious flier, or "Just my luck, it'll get stuck," for the anxious elevator traveler. I realized that Dan needed to learn how to slow down the racing "what ifs."

A New Perspective

In my twelve sessions with Dan, we worked on possibilities and probabilities, focusing on every issue he had brought up, including public transportation. Looking at the world this way gave him a whole new perspective. Though we focused on his immediate concern about getting the flu, the symptoms of his anxiety just about stopped. He was able to have a good laugh at the illogic of his "public transportation" remark. His tense posture began to relax, and his voice got calmer as he was able to process how many good environments he was actually in over the course of a day. He had a supportive workplace; he could use a car instead of public transportation; and he was provided with annual flu vaccines. All of these were beneficial to his well-being. This remarkably anxiety-filled person actually came to realize he was a lucky guy.

As our sessions came to an end, we looked back on what Dan had accomplished. We had created cognitive challenges—the concept of possibilities and probabilities—that enabled him to readjust his all-or-nothing thinking to a more moderate perspective. He had a powerful tool for facing anxiety, no matter what caused it, that he would be able to draw on long after our visits stopped. He knew how to challenge worries before they overwhelmed him. As he told me, it was like being armed with his own flu shot—or the mental equivalent. And, as he joked with me, he would not get "sick" again.

Anxiety Case Study #2: Monica and Betty: Pregnant and Anxious

A planned pregnancy should be a time of joy. But for working women in the U.S. without paid medical maternity leave, it's also a time of anxiety. This anxiety may get worse and more pronounced as the weeks progress. Along with the usual pregnancy worries about body image, the baby's health, labor, and childbirth, many women must also worry about their financial security: *What will I do about maternity leave?* A woman may be fraught with anxiety over whether having to make an impossible choice between baby and job. And all too often, women I've talked to and treated find out that they have no paid maternity leave at work. The only way to take time off is to do so under the Family Medical Leave Act, which lets some employees take up to twelve weeks of unpaid leave. But that's *unpaid* leave.

When Monica came to my office, she was pregnant with her first child. She'd been referred by her obstetrician, who was at a loss to how to help her cope with her mounting anxieties. A senior receptionist and hostess in an upscale restaurant with a large staff, Monica told me she was fraught with worries over the changes happening to her body—to an extent, being a hostess requires meticulous grooming and attention to one's appearance. She was startled enough by some of the physical, hormonal, and mental changes she was going through. But she was also constantly anxious about the ensuing conflict between working and raising her baby, and the potential financial toll that an unpaid maternity leave, necessary or not, would take on her and her husband. Like so many Americans, they were a two-income family, and even covering the basics depended on both partners working.

The restaurant Monica worked at employed several people to do the same job, often under her supervision; she had trained some of the other hostesses herself. Monica told me she was terrified that she wouldn't be able to hold onto her job after the baby came. If she stayed away too long, they would replace her. When she did return, she'd lose her standing and authority. Worse, the restaurant only offered five days of paid vacation a year. Five days was nothing after having a baby. How would she and her husband be able to cope financially if she didn't go back to work right away? But how could she manage as a new mother, with a newborn to care for, if she didn't take time off? She would have to go back to work, Monica told me, and the thought of it terrified her.

Family and friends who already had children had told her over and over that staying at home would be best for her and the baby—that they needed time get to know each other, and she would need time to recuperate and get back on her feet. Concerned as well with her own physical well-being, Monica was well aware that it takes time to recover from the stresses of childbirth. My father, who delivered many babies early in his surgical career, often said it takes at least a year for a woman's body to fully recover from this momentous experience. Anatomically and physiologically, the return to a pre-pregnancy state is slow. But the process of recovering mentally can also take a long time, and it happens gradually.

Between a Rock and a Hard Place

As our conversation proceeded, I saw that Monica really was seized with fear over her situation. She couldn't sleep at night. She was already obsessed with how much she loved her unborn son. She knew without a doubt that she wouldn't feel ready to leave him after five days, or even a couple of weeks of unpaid leave. Not only was he her first child, but all her life, growing up with two sisters, she'd been captivated by the idea of having a boy.

Her anxiety and obsessive thinking kept bringing her back to the restaurant: what would it mean to stay out for three months? She couldn't afford to lose the income, and she certainly was risking the possibility of losing her job. She was not in a union and had no job security whatsoever. And then there was the fact that she knew very well there were a number of other hostesses just waiting for her position — since she had trained them herself. The stakes were terribly high.

Helping Monica Fast

We worked together for six visits, over a period of three months. That's all it took. The first thing to do was explore Monica's past experience with anxiety: was she an anxious personality? The answer was a resounding no. She had no previous psychiatric history, felt she was in a good marriage, and in general, had that kind of social ease and upbeat personality that makes a great hostess. We also discussed how her feeling better would also have a positive effect on her baby. We talked about how to live in the here and now.

What I didn't bring up was any correlation between a mother's state of mind and the baby she was carrying. There are some indications of this: one review of 13 studies published from 1966 to 2006 found that in eight of the studies, anxiety during pregnancy was tied to prematurity and low birthweight. But Monica brought up this issue herself. And knowing that her anxiety could also be bad for the baby only added to her stress level. On top of financial hardship, she was consumed by anxiety about "what ifs." She was stuck in a vortex of fears and can't-win scenarios.

I decided to get to the core of the conflict. The truth is, Monica knew what she wanted. She wanted to stay home with her baby for at least three months. She also knew that not going back to work as soon as possible might cost her not only three months of vital income, but also her job. Two all-or-nothing concepts, neither of which allows for any flexibility — that's what seemed to be the root cause of her profound anxiety.

So first, we discussed the various "what ifs."

What if she stayed home?

What if she went back to work?

The thing about LPA is that it's flexible: it's designed to help the patient in the best way possible and as soon as possible. Monica, I realized, needed immediate help. So we shifted from the Learning phase right to the Action phase. I decided to teach her some self-hypnosis techniques right away. They would help her relax, I explained, and pointed out that they would also be of great help when she went into labor and delivery. She was excited about this and was able to relax a bit, knowing that a strategy was in place that could begin to help her.

First, I taught her a method of self-hypnosis using the eye roll technique:

• She rolled her eyes up.

• She closed her eyelids.

• Then, eyes up, eyelids closed, she took a few slow, deep breaths.

Even after the first try, Monica said she felt slightly more relaxed. We practiced this eye roll/deep breathing technique until she mastered it, and could do it with ease at home. She was good at it and really focused. I added a few cognitive strategies that involved the split-screen technique. She conjured pleasant scenes for herself and "watched" them on her own mental movie screen. Instead of a dire scenario, she could mindfully replace it with a sweet one.

Self-Hypnosis for Sleeping

To deal with Monica's insomnia, we worked on a hypnotic technique. Since she was pregnant, it was best she did not take any medications. (One note on this: to reduce an unfortunate overprescribing of sleep medications today, as discussed earlier, the American College of Physicians recently recommended CBT as the first choice in treating insomnia. No surprise to me: it's been the first choice throughout my career.) So I taught Monica to visualize twenty heavily carpeted steps (the color was her choice). Then she would picture herself walking slowly down each step, sinking deeper into this lovely, soft, and appealing carpet. By the time she reached steps 16, 17, 18, 19, and finally 20, she would be so relaxed she could fall into a comfortable sleep. She agreed to practice this at home every night. By our next visit, she had done so well at conquering her insomnia by mentally "walking down the step" that she was already more relaxed. There's nothing like a good night's sleep.

Building a New Perspective

Now Monica was relaxed enough to get to talking about some of the issues that caused her anxiety. We began talking about the importance of trying not to predict the future, or about trying to imagine the prospect of leaving her baby to return to work just so she could keep her job. I told her that yes, these were all issues she could think about, but that she could teach herself just to *think* about them and not have them dictate her life. The self-hypnosis strategy and improved sleep were already lessening her overall stress and anxiety. Now she began to work on developing a new perspective on her anxiety-driven obsessive thoughts and fears.

With that in mind, we began to explore other thoughts she had about her future and career. Was she really trapped into only one option as far as a job or a livelihood? Actually, no: she was already thinking about returning to school to study the culinary arts, and she had longed dreamed of becoming a chef and even owning a restaurant one day. Although the restaurant where she worked as a hostess was high-end, she told me that a restaurant nearby had recently offered her a job. It was part of a chain of restaurants, and she and her husband often went there. During this overwhelming period of stress and anxiety, Monica had completely forgotten about the offer. The job they had offered her would pay less, but it had more benefits and more room to grow.

And that gave her an idea: How about, after the baby was born, she followed up on this possibility? And with some discussion back and forth (and me suggesting it might be good to not postpone looking into this), she realized there was no reason to wait—she could certainly begin to look into it now. I pointed out that part of this therapy, and part of life, is learning to move away from all-or-nothing thinking. That's where she had become trapped. Her freedom, and all of ours as well, lies in being able to have a broader view of what's possible.

Monica did interview for the new job. She was hired for a part-time position with a start date of her choosing, and wound up having a lovely, healthy baby. In the interim, her husband was able to pick up some overtime work to make up for some of the family's financial loss. All in all, a happy ending and a new beginning. In a relatively short period of time, by re-thinking and restructuring ideas and perspectives, Monica was able to find freedom fast — without having to undergo an arduous phase of traditional talk therapy or divert her attention to multiple issues of her life and upbringing in order to dredge up the deeper meanings of her anxiety. All this would have done is leave her without a way to resolve the very specific issue she sought help for. Instead, she got what she needed.

Betty: The Pressure of a Power Suit

Monica's financial situation was obviously a big factor in her anxiety issues, but job-related anxiety can also affect pregnant women with high-paying careers and generous maternity benefits. I worked with a patient named Betty who was an attorney at a prosperous Wall Street law firm. Well-groomed and always dressed in tailored, expensive power suits, she was the very image of a successful lawyer. Her firm offered several months of maternity leave, but the culture of the office wasn't exactly friendly to pregnant mothers-to-be. Her colleagues, nearly all men, and many fathers themselves, frequently made jokes and uncomfortable remarks about her pregnancy—but suddenly, she didn't feel like one of the guys.

I couldn't do anything about her coworkers' insensitivity. But I could help Betty cope with her own anxiety. She was extremely fearful about the consequences of stepping away from her job for such a long time, though she had the right to maternity leave. She was convinced that a long time away from the office would negatively affect her relationship with her boss and her standing at the firm. Her goal was to become a partner. And how would she be able to balance the responsibilities of career and new motherhood?

Betty's anxiety had become so acute that her doctor referred her to me for treatment. Without medication, and in a short amount of time, she made great progress working with LPA and relaxation techniques. Like Monica, she learned to focus on where her feet were, so to speak, and not give in to the frightening litany of "what if's." We went over her law school career, including her being on law review, being hired by a top firm and all the successful cases she had completed. Refocusing on her personality assets and strengths helped her refocus again on who and what she is. And by so doing, we were able to have her move away from focusing on the terrifying anxieties of dealing with this male-dominated law firm. In the process, she did recall that there were actually a number of very supportive men out there, something she had forgotten about during her periods of overwhelming anxiety. These are practical tools that helped both women cope with new motherhood and parenting as well.

Anxiety Case Study #3: Jerome: Anxious, Depressed, and Obsessed

When anxiety co-exists with other disorders, it can be a challenge to know where to begin.

I once treated a dentist named Jerome who also coached Little League. He came to me angry, anxious, and depressed all at once. But most of all, his anxiety was off the walls. Why? Because, he told me, he could not get his Little League team to arrive on time for practices. Sometimes players were even late for their games. Jerome was a perfectionist, something he admitted to me. When the young players' parents didn't pick them up promptly after a game or practice, it bothered him even more. In fact, he told me, it was downright unacceptable and anxiety and stress would overcome him.

To say Jerome had high standards would be an understatement. In his case, his expectations were absolutely toxic: they were impossible to meet, a fact that triggered deep and lasting bouts of anger when his anxiety was out of control. It's not uncommon for some people who get anxious to project their anxiety onto others. Apparently, Jerome's anxiety and subsequent rage was also ruining life at home. He was making his whole family miserable. Every time he came home from a game or a practice, he was in a terrible mood. His wife finally put her foot down: she'd had enough of his explosions and contagious unhappiness. Either he could get professional help, or his life was about to change profoundly.

It's Their Fault

When, at our first meeting, I asked Jerome why he thought he needed help, he immediately explained that it was at his wife's insistence. He could even explain that she was tired of his being so anxious, stressed-out and depressed. It was clear he was anxious, and depressed as well. But his interpretation of what caused all this was the interesting part. His blow-up about his young players being late was the last straw as far as his wife was concerned. But Jerome didn't see it that way.

"None of this would have happened if those kids were on time," he said. "It's their fault."

His response was a sign of something else: a kind of rigid thinking and attention to every last detail. As he talked about the incidents that had made him so angry, he returned again and again to everyone else. He could remember exactly how many minutes late each player had been to each practice, what that player had said, how he had responded, and what should have happened. Jerome was keeping score.

Signs of an Obsessive-Compulsive Personality

His dogged attention to detail, critical analysis of his own behavior and that of others, plus a need to be in almost absolute control of his environment, pointed to one thing: Obsessive-Compulsive Personality Disorder, or OCPD as well as all his anxieties.

OCPD is defined by an obsessive attention to detail and, often, rigid thinking. It shares some similarities with Obsessive-Compulsive Disorder, or OCD, in which obsessive thought patterns and compulsive behavior patterns (such as counting steps, putting on clothes in exactly the same order, and other rituals) dominate everyday life. But using the term "OCD" as slang for someone who's uptight misses how harmful this condition can be — and misses the distinctions between the two as well.

People with OCPD, like Jerome, are compelled to be in control and convinced they know best. They're micro-managers. They always have to be right. But they are also beset by an endless sequence of "should have, would have, could have" thoughts. It's what the well-known 20th-century psychiatrist Karen Horney called "the tyranny of the shoulds." Jerome exhibited all of these behaviors, along with the anxiety and depression that had brought him to my office.

Working with Jerome

Jerome's perspective made it difficult, at first, to reach him. During our first evaluation visit, he kept referring to me as a psychologist.

I clarified, telling him that I was a psychiatrist, and explaining the distinctions between the two professions. But he wouldn't be convinced. He found different ways to hold onto his own notion in a manner that made him correct in his mind, though clearly, he knew the difference.

Next, we discussed the timeframe for working together. I suggested a three-month block, adding that if he felt better or wanted to leave before the three months were over, it would be no problem. His immediate response was true to form. He contradicted my suggestion, saying he wanted to work in *two*-month blocks. So I agreed immediately. My agreement was intended to make a point: I wasn't rigidly wedded to my plan. It took him aback. By agreeing with him without hesitation, I was modeling how easy it can be to give up control of things that really don't matter that much.

Over the course of eight visits, Jerome and I discussed many other issues that frustrated him. He was irritated by his dental lab technician's inefficiency. By the local school system's inability to get anything right. By pretty much everything. He had an unshakeable, rigid belief system in which he was right and they were wrong. The problem he kept going back to was not his. It was theirs. He was right, and they were wrong. He was the organized and rational one. They were the opposite.

Jerome Learns

Many theories aim to explain Obsessive-Compulsive Personality Disorder, ranging from the psychoanalytic ideas of Dr. Sigmund Freud and Dr. Wilhelm Reich to the interpersonal analytic theories of Dr. Harry Stack Sullivan. The behaviorists focused on poor learning that reinforces behavioral characteristics of OCPD. So I decided to focus on the learning aspect of my Learning, Philosophizing, and Action (LPA) technique.

Again and again, I encouraged Jerome to focus on the fifteen players on his Little League team. I got him to think about the broader context in which these fifteen players lived. Since they were too young to drive, we figured out that those fifteen players' trips to the playing field probably involved their parents and other family members, which might add up to a hundred or more people.

Then I had him think about the parents. There were at least twenty-five working parents involved. They had jobs and colleagues. There were probably at least a few divorces, which would mean more than just fifteen households. There might be various brothers and sisters who also needed rides. What else might we add to this mix of variables? I had Jerome add all of these factors into his coaching framework. He did a great job at figuring it all out.

But when I jokingly proposed that I take over the team—since, clearly, he was so frustrated with it—Jerome objected. That would be impossible, he said. I did not live in his town, or know the players and their extended families, so how could I possibly understand the parameters of coaching the team? The transportation variables "he" had figured out were very complicated, and needed time and flexibility. And as he explained all that to me, he said, "You know, I might be getting it." He was starting to understand the many conditions and variables that affected his team.

Now I shifted back to his original insistence on referring to me as a psychologist rather than a psychiatrist, even though I kept reminding him I was a psychiatrist. Jerome's thinking opened up a bit more. He knew my educational background, because I had explained it. But due to the nature of his own personality, it was very hard for him to admit that such definitions did not make a dent in his own rigid thinking. "Well," I said, "You're not a periodontist, are you?" No, he said, he was not. He was a dentist, and it wasn't the same thing. I took heart in knowing that Jerome had made some progress. He was starting to have some perspective about his rigid thinking and dogmatism. At this point, his family dynamics at home began to improve as well.

Building a Partnership

My goal with Jerome was to first establish a therapeutic alliance, which I did. I wanted to help him understand (which is very different than simply disagreeing with someone) that there are many variables in almost any situation. And there are many different ways to solve problems, from the rigid and concrete to the more speculative and abstract. In treating patients with enormous amounts of anxiety coupled to personality issues, in this case OCPD, the question is how to help these uptight people loosen up and stop punishing themselves and those around them. Often, that's what leads to the anxiety, stress, and depressive symptoms that bring them in for help. In Jerome's case, his anxiety and depression stemmed from his obsessive thinking. So that's what we worked on.

Jerome continued to want all of his ducks in a row. That was just a part of the way he saw the world. He functioned much better when people around him were organized and on time. But still, he became far more accepting of the notion that other people might have other realities. A child might be late because his parent got stuck at work, or the car was having problems. He got that. And he also became better at of problem solving. He softened up instead of getting angry. He developed a sense of compassion, which became very clear when one of his dental patients was in distress on a weekend and he could offer assistance and alter what he was doing. He could then transfer that new understanding into other areas. He could imagine reasons for things not working out exactly as he wanted them to, just like a toothache or gum abscess could occur on a weekend. He became more flexible, and that flexibility could be applied to other aspects of his life. This meant that not only would life get better for him, it would also get better for his Little League team. And, perhaps most importantly, for his wife.

Anxiety Case Study #4: Lauren: An Anxiety-Ridden Physics Professor, Plagued by Imaginary Locusts

Lauren's anxiety was overwhelming due to one obsessive thought, and it was a waking nightmare. In it, she was being destroyed by a plague of locusts, much like the one that had attacked Egypt in Biblical times. Repeated endlessly in her mind, the anxiety of this horrifying thought had become so vivid over the years that living with it had become almost unbearable.

By all outside indicators, Lauren was a successful professional: a physics professor at a prestigious West Coast university. Before earning her PhD, she had graduated from a Seven Sisters college. Over the years, she had raised two children, now successful young adults and negotiated a thorny divorce, all the while continuing to excel at her job. She was smart and competent and she was also anxiety ridden, and tormented by visions of locusts.

Therapeutic Misses

When Lauren first decided she needed professional help for this recurring, anxiety/obsessive vision, she entered twice-weekly psychotherapy. During those sessions, she discovered a lot about herself. For one thing, she realized she had always been far more organized than most of her peers. As a child, she had behaved in some ways like a little adult. And she'd also addressed many of her own issues of shame, guilt, rage, and despair. Some of these stemmed from childhood, some were due to a tough divorce. The therapist had cautioned that medication would mask the root problem but not solve it, so she hadn't taken anything. And five years later, despite all the valuable self-exploration she'd accomplished, she was still plagued by terrifying anxiety and visions, obsessed with the fear that locusts would surround and attack her.

Next, she went to a psychiatrist. This doctor assured her that medications were safe, and put her on a tricyclic antidepressant that was designed to target obsessive thoughts. And yes, Lauren's obsessive thoughts did become less frequent. But they were no less intense. Furthermore, she was having trouble coping with the side effects of the medication. So her psychiatrist switched her to an SSRI (selective serotonin reuptake inhibitor)—a class of medication that includes such familiar names as Zoloft, Paxil, and Prozac. But they were no more successful.

Lauren was at the end of her rope. That's when she decided to head east, to try a "geographic cure." Maybe, she reasoned, if she got away from the wide-open spaces of her California home, she could also escape the visions of locusts. Her decision wasn't without precedent: in the past, people who could afford it would "take a cure" in far-flung locales to recuperate and heal after a traumatic event. So Lauren took a sabbatical from her university, and relocated to New York City. No arid plains or wide-open spaces, no desert, no farm fields —none of the environmental conditions that are associated with biblical tales of those awful plagues of locusts. But there they were. Still terrifying. And that's when she was referred to me.

Getting to Work

As always, I took a thorough history. Lauren talked about her earlier bouts with therapy, and she explained how she'd gained insight into her own personality. She relayed more facts of her life: a comfortable middle-class childhood, a marriage that had lasted until the children were grown and then crumbled into divorce. She seemed to have a good sense of who she was: an accomplished intellectual and academic, a mother whose daily life functioned pretty well—so long as she wasn't experiencing the bouts of anxiety and obsessive thoughts that literally plagued her. I agreed with her assessment of herself, and admired her self-esteem, which I told her. I explained the treatment I had in mind: three or four sessions lasting ninety minutes each.

Four sessions? Lauren was astonished. She was skeptical. How could any short-term treatment help her overcome a problem she'd struggled with for so many years? How could it do what two rounds of therapy and various pharmaceuticals couldn't? Since she was desperate for relief, she agreed to give it a shot. After all, we reasoned, what did she have to lose? I was simply offering what I do in these cases and did not want to embark on other traditional treatments that had already failed her.

I explained to Lauren that I planned to apply two concepts to treat her obsessive thoughts, which needed to be treated in order to deal with her overwhelming anxiety. First was the possibility and probability concept—certainly a way of thinking that she, as a scientist, could relate to. It took us half an hour to cover this.

There was certainly a *possibility* that a plague of locusts could attack her.

But was it probable? Was it actually probable, here in New York City? On, say, a subway platform?

No, she admitted. And saw the humor in it as well.

Next, we discussed Newton's third law of motion, a basic principle familiar to anyone who's ever taught (or taken) an introductory course in physics: For every action, there is an equal and opposite reaction. When translated into Lauren's personalized treatment strategy, this became "For every thought, there is an equal and opposite thought."

Lauren easily accepted that theory. It helped to relieve the anxiety of her obsessive thoughts. Taken further, that concept evolved into accepting that for every thought there can be a *lesser* though—and possibly, even *no* thought. I've found over the years that the "no-thought" concept can help patients get long-term relief from an obsessive thought that has become extremely destructive. Sometimes I talk patients through a hierarchy of obsessive and distressful thoughts. But Lauren already understood it and had a sense of where I was going. We practiced these thoughtful mental exercises over and over again in the few visits we had, as well as Lauren reviewing these newer concepts and changing perception on her own.

No More Locusts, No More Anxiety

By the time Lauren returned to her home in California, she was able to pick up her thriving and demanding academic career free of that terrifying obsessive thought: the locusts were gone. She did continue to take the SSRI under the care of the psychiatrist who had first prescribed it. The combination proved effective, in the same way that taking a medication aimed at reducing cholesterol works best when coupled with positive changes in diet and exercise routines. But for Lauren, the best news of all was being able to drive past the wide-open meadows of her home state without seeing even a hint of a swarm.

She was free.

PART THREE

Post-Traumatic Stress Disorder

CHAPTER 10

PTSD, Hiding in Plain Sight

At any given time, on any given day in the United States, about 8 percent of the entire population is suffering from PTSD. Unfortunately, many of them are misdiagnosed with other disorders. As I write this, we've got soldiers involved in all manner of military operations and conflicts, under intensely heavy, traumatic stress. I have nothing but respect for what they do, and both personal and professional empathy for their situation. But in this section, I'm talking about non-combat PTSD. I'm talking about the kind of PTSD that afflicts many of us—due to catastrophic events such as manmade or natural disasters, torture, abuse, or any number of traumatic events that may threaten one's very existence; threaten the environment around us, or threaten the existence of a loved one, and as I've seen, more commonly, lesser personal disasters such as job loss, certain family issues, or severe financial setbacks. These events may be theoretically less devastating, but they can seriously affect a person's identity and sense of self, and can ravage that person's peace of mind. And yet they're rarely factored in as PTSD events, where often they belong.

I like to call this **sub-threshold PTSD**. It can exist below the threshold of what the psychiatric and medical establishment define as causes of PTSD, but there is no doubt it's PTSD. Many times, it turns out that the patient is suffering from PTSD, but it went overlooked and undiagnosed, because the problems they faced were not life threatening. They weren't in wars. They hadn't been nearly murdered.

Yet, brains don't make these clinical distinctions, and that's key here. So, too, is the fact that each and every brain processes information differently — so emotional and intellectual memories will be quite different depending on who we are. There are plenty of problems that our brains may process as the "end of the world" even if they aren't, such as a divorce, having to move, losing a job, a terrible breakup, bankruptcy, a fender-bender car accident, the loss of a pet. Wrongly and simplistically diagnosed as suffering from event-induced anxiety, many patients are poorly treated, and do not get better. Now, fortunately, the therapeutic community is waking up. Still, few in that community know how to use the best treatments available for treating PTSD—which are most often not medications. Time and again, experts in treating PTSD recommend medication and barely emphasize non-medicinal care.

In my experience, back in the 1970s and 80s, learning from one of my great teachers, Dr. Herbert Spiegel, the best treatments were non-medicinal. I've used and developed these approaches, including LPA, over the course of many years, and I have found they work far better than medications.

The most recently updated federal clinical practice guidelines advocate psychotherapy ahead of medication as the recommended first line of treatment. Dr. Lori L. Davis, a clinical professor of psychiatry and behavioral neurobiology at the University of Alabama, coauthored the guidelines—based on evidence gathered through March of 2016. According to the update, the Department of Veterans Affairs and the Department of Defense strongly recommend individualized, manualized trauma-focused psychotherapy over pharmacology — except when such therapy is not available. And the report describes therapy as including a number of different forms of prolonged exposure therapy, CBT, and eye movement desensitization methods. It's a terrific step in the right direction.

A Sad Gap in Treatment

One of the saddest aspects of PTSD is that so often the people who suffer live essentially "in their own heads" with the trauma, as the intrusive memories go around and around, and more and more social isolation sets in. The medications available may help someone once in a while, but at this point medications are rarely successful. And what's worse is that many of these people are receiving medications once a month, with no support in between. A key part of healing PTSD is becoming active—socially and physically—getting out in the world and getting the brain to focus on something else. Just like someone stuck in his own feedback loop of regrets and bad memories—a "could've/would've/should've" rut —PTSD sufferers spend their lives endlessly reliving past experiences. Their circuitry is stuck, in a sense, reliving a trauma over and over.

But when a PTSD sufferer is treated in one of the rethinking, re-learning, and positive exposure therapies, such as LPA, not only is the therapy more effective, but the regular weekly or biweekly therapeutic visits are a way to counteract the terrible social isolation so often present in PTSD.

Out of a Hurricane: Insights on PTSD

Remarkably, PTSD was not even recognized as a viable disorder with specific symptoms that could be reliably diagnosed until 1980. And they still don't have it right. Not surprisingly, you can add hurricanes to the long, long list of its causes. Actually, a hurricane — and its effect on me – is what made me realize when writing this book that I had to include PTSD. Looking back on it, the story is filled with cues that I could have ended up with a form of PTSD — mild, to be sure, but mystifying and pernicious. It might have crept up on me gradually, but left me to rethink my own vulnerabilities. And it gave me invaluable insight into why PTSD and its symptoms are so often misread, misdiagnosed, and mistreated, if they're treated at all.

It was fall, 2012. Hurricane Sandy was headed for New York City. So I prepared: I stocked up on food, water, and batteries, checked my flashlights and got out the battery-powered radio. I had a go-bag packed with essentials, just in case.

At the time, I was in midtown Manhattan, where I could see the NYU Langone Medical Center, where I trained, and ran the short-term psychotherapy program for twenty years. It's a place that's been such a huge part of my life. It's a big facility, with offices for the staff at NYU Medical Center, a bustling emergency room, and the capacity to care for and house hundreds of patients. It's also got research labs, a teaching campus, a housing complex, and a huge staff. It has its own generators. And it's nestled close to the East River, with a clear view of the water — which, until Hurricane Sandy, was quite a plus.

This was a familiar neighborhood, and I'd known many of my neighbors. In the hours before the storm, we passed each other doing errands and gathering supplies. Some people were especially worried about the storm, they told me, and in my usual way, I offered comfort. I felt secure in some kind of knowledge that we were going to be all right. Our city is remarkable, I noted. And I'd prepared well, according to what the mayor and governors of New York, New Jersey, and Connecticut had told us all to do. This is a self-sufficient city, after all. What could happen?

That night, Monday, October 29, the storm hit with a vengeance. At 8:30, the lights in our building dimmed for a moment and then got bright again. Looking out the window, I saw that lights at one of the medical center housing complexes had gone out. The lights flickered on, then off again in the medical center. But why weren't the hospital's generators kicking on?

Twenty minutes later, my building's power went out as well. "Not going to worry," I told myself. After all, all the power lines in the city are underground.

A neighbor came by, flashlight in hand. We stood in my darkened kitchen, and I offered him a glass of water. "Maybe you shouldn't run the water," he said. Without electricity, the water stops too, as the pumps in the basement can't run. Still, I said, "They'll have it fixed soon. This is New York City."

The hours passed, and the storm continued to batter my city. In my darkened apartment, I checked the food and water in my refrigerator—still cold. I tuned into an all-talk news station on my battery-operated radio. Evening turned into night, and the news began to get worse. There was a massive explosion at the ConEdison electric plant on 14th Street, leaving hundreds of thousands without power. It wasn't just a few buildings that were dark, it was the entire lower portion of Manhattan island—including my neighborhood. No traffic lights, no open food stores, no operating gas stations, and soon, the emergency lights—only good for two hours—went out in the halls and stairwells of my building, leaving everything pitch black. It was as if the city went dead.

Then the sirens started. I looked out the window at flashing lights. There were ambulances lining up in front of the NYU Medical Center. The hospital was being evacuated; it was flooded, the power was out. The generators weren't working, so neither were the lights or elevators. The hospital staff, EMS workers, firemen and police officers were getting hundreds of patients out—carrying them down stairways, setting them up in ambulances, and sending them to other hospitals that hadn't been hit as hard.

It was harrowing, and heartbreaking on so many levels. This was my hospital—where I had trained, treated patients, and supervised residents, where my sons were born, where my surgeon father died, where all six of my grandchildren were born—an institution I know inside and out, a place where I have lifelong friendships and professional relationships, and I know what it means to have to evacuate patients. I felt like I was witnessing the downfall of a bedrock in my life. But I was also stricken with concern for the patients and staff.

I slept very little that night, wondering if there was anything I could do. The evacuations went on all night and into the next day, and I kept watch from my window. In the building, the electricity was still off — as it was all over downtown. The food was going to spoil in the fridge, the cell phone was out of power, there was no water, the bathroom wasn't working. I began to feel a sense of despair and frustration. My spirits got low.

The next day, we all learned it would be days before power could be restored. The city was in tatters. I felt the storm had won. Though I had insisted to my sons (one of whom still had power in his home) that I was going to be fine, I changed my mind by Day Three. Luckily, the landline still worked.

"You all right?" said my son at my call.

"Come get me," I said.

Getting down the stairs with a flashlight and a suitcase was hard. I felt lightheaded. I was dehydrated. I'm not young. At one point, as my hands reached for the banister while trying not to lose the flashlight or drop my suitcase, I nearly lost my footing. I caught myself just before falling. I would have tumbled down a flight. My heart was pounding with anxiety. I was physically and emotionally drained. I was also unhappy. I was angry that this could happen in a city like New York. How could the electrical company not have foreseen this possibility when they built the power plant along the East River? Why hadn't they thought about the river flooding over the walls? Why hadn't they prepared? I had a creeping sense of discouragement.

I'm relating this because all of these feelings gave me a sharp sense of clarity into what happens to us in the face of trauma, and how one single event can bring on PTSD. I felt this from a far more direct vantage point than I ever had in all of my practice, or my life. I wasn't there to help someone who was feeling this way; *I* was feeling this way. It was only when I was safely sitting with my family at my son's home that the magnitude of Hurricane Sandy became clear.

Like so many, I could not tear myself away from the tragedies reported on television, an endless stream of destruction and loss: businesses, property, lives. People were injured, dying, dislocated, dazed. I felt both lucky and hopeless. And after two days holed up in my apartment, watching a giant institution brought to its knees and unable to do anything to help, watching vulnerable, fragile patients loaded into ambulances, I felt fragile and vulnerable myself.

My own life had been changed. I certainly would not be able to go into work; there was no way to get there, and it would be awhile before transportation was back on its feet. Further, the hospital—my hospital, my second home – was devastated. I felt a pressing need to regroup my senses and emotions. I *had* to check out. I began to feel as if I had caught the virus of despair that was afflicting so many of us.

That's when I began to think of the PTSD patients I've treated using non-medicinal approaches—and the psychological toll that Hurricane Sandy was already having on so many. It reminded me of other disasters I'd witnessed from the TV, if only from an intact environment: 9/11, Hurricane Katrina, the earthquake in Haiti, and the BP oil spill—to name just a few disasters, both natural and manmade — would inevitably lead to numerous PTSD cases. What is needed, I thought (and still do), was a clear understanding that PTSD may not be completely obvious at first, and it may not be the same for everyone, but it has to be treated --- and the sooner, the better. Left alone, it may worsen.

One key here is that it is far better to tackle PTSD as soon as you notice it, before it becomes an established pattern in the brain, and before that way of thinking is so well incorporated into your way of thinking that it's no longer unusual. Sadly, for those left untreated, PTSD starts to feel normal. But treating it takes a very specific approach. I use a tried and true treatment process that has been quite successful with my PTSD patients: Prolonged Exposure Therapy, or Guided Imagery. This method was first developed by Dr. Joseph Wolpe in the mid-twentieth century.

Dr. Wolpe demonstrated that, all too often, stress, anxiety, and traumatic experiences are incompatible with pleasant visualizations. This method, a process that builds up as the patient gets better, not only works in an office setting but can also be modified and practiced at home or work in a matter of seconds or minutes. I'll show some powerful examples of how it works in the case studies in this chapter.

A Severe Emotional Response — to Life

Let me step back a bit to offer some history. The roots of how PTSD was discovered actually helped make it harder to recognize and understand. And remember, the psychiatric establishment didn't even include PTSD in the *DSM* until 1980.

During the Civil War, an internist named Jacob Mendes Da Costa, who was serving as an assistant surgeon in the U.S. Army, noticed that many soldiers were complaining of similar heart symptoms. Soldiers were coming to him for relief from chest pains, palpitations, and shortness of breath. Many said that when they had to march uphill or prepare for battle, they couldn't keep up and would feel extremely winded.

This set of symptoms became known as Da Costa's Syndrome, and was thought to be related to anxiety. It was found among soldiers in other wars as well. Again, no cardiac illness was found. It was also known as soldier's heart, shell shock, combat neurosis, and (as my own father called it) anxiety neurosis. In World War II, it was also known as battle fatigue, as doctors began to realize that any soldier could get it from the stresses of battle, as well as reaching a point of physical, mental, and emotional exhaustion which could also cripple a man—or a woman—for life. Interestingly, in the *Journal of Early Science and Medicine* (2014.19 (6) 549–57), Abdul Hamid and Jamie Hacker Hughes published findings of an Assyrian text from a Mesopotamian (presently Iraq) study that described PTSD symptoms in soldiers such as sleep disturbances, flashbacks, and "low mood," similar to some of the symptoms we describe today as PTSD as early as 1,300 BC. However, it should be kept in mind that describing and analyzing symptoms so many thousands of years ago to a more recent medical or psychiatric disorder is far from clear and may involve many other medical and even cultural issues. What does seem clear is that PTSD is not just a modern disorder, but no doubt goes back many centuries as a human issue.

Among Vietnam veterans, PTSD was an epidemic: 30 percent of all American soldiers were affected with severe symptoms, and another

25 percent were affected at the subclinical level, where the symptoms were not as overt. And 13 percent of all veterans from the Iraq and Afghan wars have been diagnosed with PTSD. In addition, after the attack on the World Trade Center on September 11, 2001, found 11.4% of survivors suffered from PTSD and 9.7% from depression (Sadock, *Sadock and Ruiz; Synopsis of Psychiatry,* 11th Edition, 2015.)

These statistics speak to such a prevalence of this disorder that you might call PTSD a problem of our society. While one organization puts it at 8 percent, another asserts that it's more like 9 to 15 percent of the general population in the United States who will get PTSD in their lifetime — potentially millions and millions of people. Add another 5 to 15 percent of the population who will suffer from subclinical versions of PTSD, and that's an enormous group of people suffering. And so many are misdiagnosed or go undiagnosed altogether.

Interestingly, research shows that about 30 percent of PTSD includes dissociation disorders, such as:

- DID, dissociative identity disorder (a kind of multiple personality disorder)
- Depersonalization, which involves feelings of detachment from people and the world around you, as if you're watching a movie
- Derealization, when it feels like the people and things around you aren't real
- Dissociative amnesia, when you can't remember key things about yourself (taken from: http://www.nami.org/Learn-More/Mental-Health-Conditions-Dissociative-Disorders).

Another important piece of research has shown that children who experience PTSD before the age of eleven are more likely to experience a PTSD response as adults. One of the case studies that follow, Sam Escapes the Nazis, describes this phenomenon.

CHAPTER 11

Treating PTSD: Therapeutic Procedures

For more than forty years of working with patients, including many with PTSD, I've been trying to come up with a term that covers what I do. And it was in writing this book that I found it. I call it "Therapeutic Procedures."

When I started my career treating people who wanted to stop smoking and lose weight, and then branched into treating phobias, anxieties, and PTSD, I called my method a "Procedure," since it's not unlike what surgeons do. That's consistent with my medical heritage: as you'll recall, my father and uncle were surgeons. Yes, it's therapeutic. But it's not an endless, open-ended, long-term state of therapy. It's fast, it's specific, and it's short-term, like many a surgical procedure. Which also means that it usually works. And if it doesn't, you repeat it, just as specifically. There's a protocol, there's a functional approach, and it is not a shot in the dark. It's based on a therapist's skill at quickly pinpointing a way into the problem and very focused ways of dealing with that problem.

But an ongoing problem with my field is that, despite all the established protocols for treating mental disorders, including PTSD, those protocols are often not followed. For example, lecture after lecture from experts in treating PTSD focuses on medications, which at this time rarely work. To make matters even worse, these same "experts" point to Cognitive Behavioral Therapy and Exposure Therapy (which exposes the patient to various levels of the trauma through hierarchy of controlled visualizations) as the best method of treatment. Talk about a disconnect. If this is the best method, where are the experts in these techniques? I've asked many of my colleagues over the years: If it's been shown that CBT and Exposure Therapies are more effective than medication and long-term talk therapy, then why aren't we, as a field, treating these patients with the protocols that show the most promise of working?

The answer, in most cases, is that my colleagues don't do that type of work. They weren't trained in it. Which means the vast majority of therapists are still either prescribing ineffective medications, or listening harder and longer and getting nowhere—or both. That is, until the patient or client stops showing up, since nothing is making a difference. Which essentially means that patient or client is *resisting* the very thing he needs—therapy. It's just that he is being treated with the wrong kind of therapy.

The problems with how we treat PTSD are many. It's underestimated as rampant in civilian as well as military life; people are getting the wrong kinds of treatment, and in some cases, their symptoms are being misread. People who suffer from PTSD are often sad — they're reliving terrible traumas, so who wouldn't be sad about that? — but they are being misdiagnosed as having depression or anxiety disorders, which can be part of PTSD, instead of PTSD.

It's an enormous disconnect, in my mind. And with PTSD, it's especially tragic. As the brain processes a loss of a job or a marriage as a form of death, it reacts in kind. For some people, the brain doesn't really make a distinction between someone saying, "I'm leaving you" or "Sorry, but we're going to have to let you go," and someone putting a gun to your head. Then, because of faulty approaches on the part of a large portion of the psychiatric/therapeutic community, the brain is not only allowed to react to that trauma, but the continued reaction increases its intensity, as the patterns are etched into the brain over time. In other words, we don't stop it, so it gets worse and worse. And that is really a shame. If, indeed, we all had a set of clear protocols for treating PTSD that we were actually trained to use and could follow, I can assure you that there would be a whole lot less PTSD.

How PTSD is Defined

My father—an eye surgeon, as I've mentioned—used the term "neurocirculatory asthenia" to include patients with visual problems if he had a hunch their eyes were not the primary issue. The problems with their eyes were, he believed, secondary to severe emotional stress. These patients were so stressed out they literally could not see straight. They were manifesting, in physical form, a severe emotional reaction to life events. This was before 1980, when the American Psychiatric Association finally classified PTSD as a disorder in the new edition of its treatment bible, the *DSM-III*. Consider that PTSD was identified as a set of symptoms during the Civil War, but it wasn't even defined until more than a hundred years later, and you have a sense of how imprecise our approach to it has been.

The *DSM-III* defined PTSD as a specific group of symptoms, or a collection of stress reactions, including:

- Increased heart rates and hyperactivity of the sympathetic nervous system
- Anxiety states and nervousness
- Recurrent thoughts and intrusive recollections of traumatic events
- Nightmares
- Flashbacks to traumatic events
- Avoidance of certain people and places
- Deterioration of interpersonal relationships
- Insomnia
- Irritability
- Emotional detachment
- Anger, shame, and guilt
- Concentration difficulties

- Depression
- Suicidal thoughts and attempts

These are all symptoms that may occur — they don't have to all occur to recognize that a patient has PTSD. But the important thing is that, as of 1980, we now had an official, clinical acknowledgment of PTSD.

In the *DSM-5*, as updated in 2013, PTSD has been given a separate classification under Trauma and Stressor-Related Disorders. However, now it is defined as something that can happen even *without* an obvious life-threatening situation depending on how each and every brain processes traumatic events and information. The idea is that PTSD and its symptoms could occur in a whole range of variations, from intense to hidden and subtle; from overt to mystifying, as I would see it. In my mind this new, expanded DSM definition was a good expansion of the disorder, but it's not there yet. Now, we could start working on treating it.

PTSD and Health Setbacks

I've treated many patients for PTSD who had suffered from a health setback. Whether it was Lyme Disease, cancer, a stroke, a stay in intensive care, or a heart attack, they wound up with a very unexpected case of PTSD. They may have been surprised, but those around them weren't. A serious illness or injury can be a key trigger.

How It Happens

The trauma—the fear and feeling of lack of control, the experience of a hospital stay, the memory of pain—can build up inside. Patients may downplay their feelings, because after all, they are "better," or just have to deal with it; the illness has to become part of their life. But they're suffering. When they come to see me, it's often at the recommendation of a doctor or therapist who realizes that their post-traumatic stress disorder was triggered by their illness. Sadly, this kind of PTSD is often overlooked, or misdiagnosed as anxiety or depression. But without treatment, symptoms worsen, affecting the sufferer's social, family, and work relationships. When you consider that some of these loved ones may have helped the patient get through his or her illness, injury or hospital stay, they may have little tolerance for this apparently erratic behavior. And then you've got a whole other level of hurt on your hands.

The Warning Signs

If you've been treated for a serious illness, health condition or injury, pay attention. PTSD can lurk in your system, and it won't necessarily happen overnight or even in a matter of days. It can strike weeks, months, or even years after you've been injured or sick. If you've been hospitalized or wound up in the ICU, you may start experiencing the symptoms of PTSD so long after the event that you don't connect them. In fact, 25 percent of those admitted to a hospital ICU will have symptoms of PTSD after their stays ("PTSD Common in ICU Survivors," *Johns Hopkins News and Publication*, April 2015), and one in eight, or 12 percent, of heart attack sufferers develop PTSD. That group is also more likely to have a second heart attack ("Heart Attack Can Trigger PTSD," Harvard Medical School, *Harvard Health Publishing*, June 25, 2012). The PTSD is more than just unpleasant emotions: it can trigger a vicious cycle of symptoms, as the heart attack survivor goes into a state of panic upon feeling short of breath, reaching a dangerous level of stress. So treating the PTSD is important for both emotional and health reasons.

So be on the lookout for:
- Nightmares
- Flashbacks
- Irritability
- A sense of detachment from yourself or a sense that things around you are changed or different (in clinical terms, we call the first state of mind *depersonalization* and the second *derealization*)

- Heightened sensitivity (for instance, to triggers such as bright lights and constant noise if you've been in the ICU)

What to Do

The good news is that I've had a lot of luck helping patients overcome illness or injury related PTSD. Actually, it has nothing to do with luck. Most of my patients are absolutely determined not to let their health setback slow them down, and they regard the related emotional setbacks the same way: let's get through it. Searching for a constructive, step-by-step way out of the PTSD is the right tactic, and if medications, after a reasonable trial, do not help (particularly SSRIs, such as Zoloft, or Paxil, as I've discussed at length), then it's time to try what has a better chance of working.

When I have a patient with this type of PTSD, the length of time it takes to break through depends on the patient, as always, and the extent of the PTSD. Sometimes all it takes is a few sessions. The most important thing is that the moment you start experience a symptom of PTSD, don't ignore it. Don't sweep it under the rug and hope it goes away. It won't. No matter which stage you're at with an illness or injury, whether fully recovered or learning how to cope with a medical condition that is now part of your life, you deserve to feel better. Also, as with any form of PTSD, no matter what the cause, the sooner you treat it, the better the outcome.

CHAPTER 12

Overcoming PTSD with LPA: Real Stories

One of the most gratifying aspects of working with PTSD patients is when I can see a patient visibly start to relax. It's as if they are emerging from the shadows. I'm including some of my most memorable examples here.

PTSD Case Study # 1: Sam Escapes the Nazis

A patient I had a few years ago, Sam, is a good example of how an illness and a hospital stay can trigger PTSD. It's also a great illustration of how someone can work through it, and overcome it, using LPA. This was a fascinating case, as here was a man who knew, rationally, that he was suffering from a total fabrication. He was desperate to break free. Our work together — and in this case, we really did collaborate — took about three months.

Sam first stepped into my office in a state of total agitation. He said there were Nazis after him. He was besieged by them. Overweight, with a pack-a-day cigarette smoking habit in the past and the tendency to work himself into exhaustion, he'd recently had a heart attack. He wound up in the hospital and then had to have an emergency bypass, and that's when the Nazis came around. During his stay in the CCU (cardiac care unit) after surgery, he had begun to dissociate and hallucinate.

Even if I'm not going down a years-long yellow brick road with a patient, it's essential to get the patient's comprehensive history. One thing that struck me right away when I was taking Sam's history was that both his parents were Holocaust survivors. As a boy in America he'd grown up listening to frequent and dramatic recollections of their harrowing experiences. These terrifying stories then became lodged in his imagination. His parents were both anxious and, understandably, still traumatized, and as a child, Sam had absorbed and internalized that anxiety and trauma. That was at the root of his very vivid and terrifying hallucinations.

Apparently, in the intensive care unit after bypass surgery, amid the bright lights and noises, the sense of tension and his own pain and discomfort, Sam's anxiety and those terrible stories he'd heard from his parents began to dig into his psyche. His Nazis were coming closer, surrounding him as he lay in his hospital bed.

Physically, Sam made a very good recovery, monitored carefully by his doctors, but mentally he was in a horrifying descent. At one point, he became so agitated that he tried to pull out his IVs, and escape by pulling himself up and over the bedrails. His sense of terror and anxiety were so bad that he had to be medicated and placed in bed restraints.

Finally, Sam had recovered enough from the surgery to be discharged from the hospital, and he was sent home. But things in his head didn't get better. The nightmare images of Nazis became a bit less frequent, but they didn't stop. And now Sam had a new problem: he was obsessed with the prospect of having another heart attack. His fear wasn't focused on the physical consequences, but on the nightmarish prospect of having to go back to the hospital and be stricken, once again, with the dissociation and hallucination that the Nazis were coming for him.

Consumed by anxiety, he isolated himself. Meanwhile, his flashbacks of being in the hospital after his heart attack and bypass surgery, plagued by his imaginary Nazis, continued to haunt him. Finally, his family suggested professional help, and his primary care doctor referred him to me.

A Perfect Storm

When Sam came to see me, it quickly became clear that the traumatic stories he had learned and absorbed in his youth had collided with a very real trauma—his heart attack and subsequent surgery and stay in the CCU—and created a perfect storm of PTSD. His parents suffered from their own PTSD, stemming from their awful experiences in the Holocaust, and in reliving them over and over with their son, they had passed their trauma on to him: the parents' nightmares had become the son's. And in the CCU, with its harsh and bright lighting and anxious atmosphere, he had dissociated into those torturous Holocaust nightmares. It felt as if they were really happening to him.

Because these memories had kept occurring after he left the hospital, I was able to rule out the effects of anesthesia or any sedative he was receiving while in the CCU. And I knew that once he started working with me, he would become less anxious and stressed, and start to improve quickly — which, in turn would help him keep practicing and progressing. The effects of LPA are reciprocal, and cumulative. I felt terrible for Sam, but I knew he was going to feel better soon. As soon as I explained that to him, he said he was already feeling a new kind of hope he hadn't in a long, long time.

Sam couldn't—and didn't—blame his parents. He understood that they had suffered terribly and had their own kind of PTSD. Since he already knew a lot about his family history, the Learning phase of LPA would take very little time. He sat in my office describing the Nazis' facial expressions and the look of their uniforms as they rounded up people, detailing scenes of people being transported in filthy railroad cars, and being tortured and killed. It was harrowing, tragic, and so vivid that, as I pointed out to him, it sounded as if he had witnessed these experiences firsthand.

Learning About the Nazis

First, we worked on Sam gaining a better understanding of how he had come to internalize his parents' terrors. These dehumanizing, awful experiences and scenes were not really his own experiences but belonged to his parents. And his parents had not meant to cause him harm: they were good people, hardworking, family oriented, and believed in the power of education and the goodness of America. And clearly, Sam had also learned a great deal about the subject of his nightmares: he was a smart boy, and a prodigious researcher. But his parents could not help reliving their awful experiences, or sharing them with their son. So a confluence had been created.

Some of what Sam had learned may have been too intense and emotional for him, so I was careful not to push for details, and just let him come to terms with it on his own. He began to see how these stories and visions had become entrenched in his psychology, creating a terribly damaging, traumatic experience. Then I started to describe the concept of faulty learning. It's not that Sam's experience was actually direct faulty learning, but more that he was absorbing what he heard around him. But faulty learning is a great way to demonstrate the power of what he had learned. For instance: What if he were my child, and I had taught him that 2+2 = 3? When he went to school, his teacher would have to spend time re-teaching him that 2+2 = 4. In a way, I suggested, it's harder to unlearn something than to learn it right the first time.

Sam had been "taught" about the Holocaust with such intensity that he actually saw *himself* as one of the victims. He learned its horrors as if he were there. And he was so profoundly affected by this learning that it became *his* story in his memory banks. Even more important, it demonstrated how complicated and powerful learning is, and how a child processes information. What's learned in childhood can affect a person's thinking and behavior straight into adulthood. In Sam's case, the realities of the Holocaust cannot be denied, of course. But it was a *learned* reality for him, not his actual experiences, that had become real to him.

When a Nightmare Takes Over Your Life

Sam learned fast. As I said, he already knew much of this, it was just a matter of guiding him to have a certain perspective on it. We went onto the next phase, Philosophizing, where we look at how what you've learned has come to affect your life. That's key: it stops your ability to have a full, happy, completely functional life, and that's why you want to feel better.

Sam and I began the Philosophizing phase by talking about his overwhelming CCU experience. It was bad enough that he had a heart attack and was in the CCU, but the whole experience was compounded by what was in his head. And this PTSD had continued into his recovery and was still affecting his life. Here he was, a happily married man with children, an MBA, and a good job as a successful office manager in a midsized law firm. Yet he was plagued by visions of Nazis. And, of course, that crippling fear: what if he had to go back to the hospital? That would be a hell inside his head.

We needed a key to unlock this trap Sam was in, and we found it in cars. He confessed to me that he felt an instinctive dislike for Germans, but he really liked German cars. My patients always surprise me—and this dichotomy was fascinating. Sam told me that he had an old Jaguar, a British car, but it wasn't reliable and he'd have to replace it soon. He was looking at Volvos (Swedish), and Lincolns (American), but he couldn't really shake the fact that deep down, what he wanted was a German car. That's what I kept in mind as we started working on how to stop Sam's terrors.

First, I suggested we talk about Germany. Why not?

"Do I have to actually *like* Germans?" he asked.

"Let's just talk about the country— but nowadays," I said, though I was pleased by his question, which showed that he was already trying to work things out rather than simply react. We philosophized about the new Germany and their democratic government, and discussed the many German-Americans who fought in WWII for the U.S. Army. The point: there was plenty that *wasn't* evil about Germany or Germans. Sam understood all of this and said he would keep thinking about it, and work on shifting his thinking and feelings. He understood that doing this was going to help him break free of his terrors.

Taking Action to Feel Better

Sam was moving fast. We were still in our first hour and a half visit when we started the Action phase of the LPA strategy. I began by teaching Sam the eyeroll hypnotic/relaxation technique I've already discussed, telling him that he could also practice this at home. Sam was eager to learn and try whatever tools he could.

I guided him through this first exercise. He sat comfortably in a chair. I asked him to roll his eyes to the top of his head, close his eyelids, and take three or four deep breaths, letting the air out slowly. As he took easy, deep breaths, he worked on relaxing his neck, back and shoulder muscles. We practiced for twenty minutes, and then he tried it on his own. Right away, he was accomplishing something—and he was cheered by this.

We then discussed how, when we connect more pleasant visualizations or thoughts to traumatic visualizations, the pleasant feeling associated with the positive image most often overcomes the stress connected to the scary one. Soon, the person feels a lot better, and is certainly in better control.

Next, we started working on a visualization technique for him. I had Sam imagine a large movie screen. On that screen, certain images that he had perceived during his CCU experience and while he was in that agitated, terrified mental state would be projected. Then I gave him his first homework assignment: to practice imagining this screen at least five to six times a day, for a minute or two —whatever time frame fit into his schedule.

Sam's second visit was much more intense. He was well practiced with imagining the screen, so we launched right into the next part of the strategy. I had Sam go into his relaxed state—using the eye-roll and deep breathing technique, and asked him to visualize the large movie screen. Then I introduced another concept. I had Sam put a line down the center of the screen, dividing it in two. I asked him to just focus on the left side of the screen, and then project certain images related to his PTSD and learned memories. But we also started with non-stressful images: the German cars he liked, for instance. He interrupted me to say he liked visualizing them.

From here we slowly moved into some of his nightmarish memories and intrusive thoughts of the Nazis surrounding and coming after him. If things became a bit too intense, I stopped, keeping those images "contained" on the left side of that imaginary split screen. The right side, we kept blank. In the meantime, we'd go back to talking about those German cars. Sam had also told me he wanted to own a fishing boat, like a Boston Whaler. I asked him to imagine it was in the water, and his whole family was out there, fishing, enjoying good times on the boat.

We went back to the screen: Now Sam was able to visualize stressful, nightmarish images of the Nazis on the left side of the screen, and then put the happier images on the right. And he could switch back and forth: Images of Nazis/Images of his family all out on the water in a magnificent boat. Images of Nazis/Images of his favorite German cars. He could choose when he wanted to switch between one side of the screen and the other. He did it at his own pace.

What we were doing was desensitizing him to the terribly intrusive thoughts and learned memories of the Holocaust by connecting them to pleasant thoughts and visualizations. And with each visit, Sam got better. He would relax nearly instantly, and conjure up the two–sided movie screen quickly. The relaxation, visualizations, and desensitization merged into one continuous process.

During our three months of treatment, we went from weekly visits for the first month to visits twice a month. Sam did more and more at home. In my office, we continued to practice and discuss issues. And he overcame the acute stress of PTSD: the nightmares and intrusive thoughts disappeared. He still remembered his childhood learning of the Holocaust and what it had done to his parents. He still admired their survival and felt compassion for them, and since we'd never once suggested that any of this was his parents' fault, his relationship with them was as strong and loving as ever. And he now had a set of techniques and strategies to control any future problems with his traumatic experiences resurfacing. As Sam left our last meeting, I was tempted to ask him if he had any plans to buy a Volkswagen or Audi. But of course, that's up to him.

PTSD Case Study #2: Gabe: The Man Who Thought He Could Fit on the Head of a Pin

Sometimes, PTSD is not the first condition I identify, but turns out to underlie some other disorder. In this case, a combination of hypnosis and LPA therapy helped me to identify the root cause of an alarming symptom my patient had lived with for twenty years, and gave him the tools to control it.

Gabe was a patient referred to me by an internist. He was a businessman in his forties, with a lifestyle that reflected his success. He liked to eat in fine restaurants and had a closet full of well-made, tailored clothes. By all outward appearances, he was a well-adjusted single man, living a life of relative comfort in the big city. He enjoyed spending a good part of the money he earned on luxuries, describing himself as a "lavish" spender on things that gave him pleasure. But inside, he was a wreck. About four or five times a day, at work and in many social settings, particularly when he was under stress, Gabe would start to feel as if he were shrinking. He would imagine himself getting smaller and smaller, until he was so tiny that he "could have fit on the head of pin," as he told me. He was a physically healthy man, and his internist felt at a loss to help him.

Simply Terrified

When Gabe first described his symptoms to me, I listened in the typical medical model of thinking, where we use all our knowledge in a process called "differential diagnosis." In other words, psychiatrists tap into our training and current research (textbooks and psychiatric journals) to create a list of possible causes that a set of symptoms may represent. In this case, with this well-organized, successful, articulate gentleman I felt comfortable ruling out any psychotic disorder. He was not delusional and was not hallucinating, there was no disorganization in his speech pattern, and he presented without signs or symptoms of a mood disorder. There was no record of head trauma. He had no history of substance abuse. Yet he was getting terrified on a regular basis from seeing himself disappear, shrinking to such a small size that he could fit on the head of a pin.

On the way to his first visit with me, Gabe had stopped at a well-known department store and bought himself a beautiful sports jacket. He had brought it with him and showed it to me as he spoke. In the middle of paying for it, he had begun to feel himself shrinking. He started to sweat, and his voice became shaky. The salesperson asked if he needed help, but he managed to snap out of it. But on the way to my office, he'd had another episode. As he said, "It happens all the time." So Gabe was really suffering, and his primary care doctor was right to refer him to me.

Unlocking a Mystery

As Gabe described his symptoms, I thought in terms of a mood disorder, such as a bipolar disorder, where a manic or hypomanic state is part of a constellation of problems, sometimes including episodes where excessive spending can be a part of the mania. Gabe had described himself as a "lavish" spender, not a diagnosis by itself, but worthy of further exploration. Was it part of a larger pattern? Where did the shrinking fit in?

As we continued our discussion, it was clear from Gabe's vivid descriptions that he did not experience the shrinking sensation as part of his imagination. But he was not under some bizarre set of obsessive delusions about the cosmos, as seen in some forms of psychosis. My impression was that he was suffering from a dissociative disorder, the major symptom being depersonalization, which is simply and clearly defined as a recurrent detachment from one's self. People going through this may feel as if they are observing themselves from the outside, as if in a movie or through the lens of a camera, or feel totally detached from who they are. Now I had two ideas: mania or hypomania, as well as a dissociative disorder. However, other than excess spending patterns, he did not appear to have any other signs or symptoms of a mood disorder. So the focus was a dissociative disorder.

This type of experience occurs more often in the general population than most people realize. Dissociative disorders are third in line after depression and anxiety disorders. Migraine sufferers may experience similar symptoms, as can people with seizure disorders and users of psychedelic drugs such as LSD and mescaline. Some head injuries can cause this phenomenon, as can sensory deprivation or traumatic experience. PTSD can also trigger a depersonalization experience, but at this point with Gabe, I was not yet considering post-traumatic stress as an explanation for his condition, which had plagued him for a torturous twenty years. Recently these episodes had been lasting longer, and becoming more frequent, than ever before. What was causing it? Could I help him?

As Gabe sat facing me, head in his hands, I felt genuinely terrible for him. He had been to many other psychotherapists, and had gotten no relief. He had been labeled a schizophrenic by one psychiatrist, who put him on antipsychotic drugs to curb his "delusions." To me this was clearly a misdiagnosis. Schizophrenia is a mental disorder often accompanied by intense delusions, voices, and hallucinations that are inconsistent with reality, but appear real to the person experiencing them. It's a serious illness and often does need medication.

Unfortunately, this psychiatrist had latched onto the notion of Gabe having delusions consistent with schizophrenia and closed off all other possibilities. All too often, many psychiatrists and even primary care doctors jump straight into the use (and often overuse) of medications, making a quick diagnosis of a disorder that might respond to medication and avoiding their own bank of knowledge and training in favor of psychopharmacology.

As mentioned earlier, too much of contemporary psychiatry has turned into medication management, where doctors are seeing three to four patients an hour, asking how they feel, checking on side effects of medications, and writing another prescription for the next month or two. This is not what mental health care is about. We should attempt to deal with the whole person and treat each patient and disorder on an individual basis.

Misdiagnosed and Still Shrinking

Gabe did not need antipsychotic medication, nor the side effects it produced. There are many reasons other than schizophrenia that could explain his symptoms, and in his case the "shrinking" phenomenon was related to a different set of circumstances. Again, he showed no signs of psychosis that would indicate schizophrenia. There were no delusions such as being paranoid (i.e. thinking water and food were poisoned) or grandiose delusions about having special powers or being groomed to run a Fortune 500 company. Nor were any of his symptoms consistent with delusions of poverty and despair that might indicate depression or a possible bipolar disorder. Yet another psychiatrist had diagnosed Gabe's problem as depression. I'd agree that experiencing an unsettling bout of watching yourself seem to shrink could indeed be quite depressing. But this particular doctor thought Gabe's lavish spending habits were his way of compensating for his inner despair.

Note that Gabe had not gone to seek any kind of help in that department. He could afford nice shoes, so he bought them. He went for help in dealing with these shrinking bouts. And while he did admit that he sometimes felt depressed, Gabe explained that if he had any concerns about his financial situation, they were more related to the economy and his fear that his business might decline—a normal issue for businessmen.

The bottom line, as I saw it, was that none of the medications he'd been prescribed had helped him in any way. All he experienced were side effects: dry mouth, lightheadedness, and constipation. The diagnosis and the medications were wrong. Furthermore, they did not help with his primary issue, the "shrinking" episodes. The mental health system had completely failed him, and he had been suffering from this complex and mystifying syndrome for far too long. At long last, his doctor had reached out to me and to an entirely different kind of treatment.

Dealing with "This Crazy Thing"

During our first visit, Gabe had described the experience of talking about himself as "okay" and made it clear that he did not want to take medications because they made him feel sick. After an hour and half, I had begun to formulate a preliminary diagnosis of a dissociative disorder with depersonalization as the main feature. In this case, micropsia (seeing altered sizes and shapes, especially of himself) was the central set of disabling symptoms that dominated the clinical picture.

When Gabe returned for a second visit, he and I talked about establishing a basis in learning for "this crazy thing," as he called it. I tried to keep my Learning, Philosophizing, and Action (LPA) technique as operative as possible to provide him with a solid learning and therapeutic matrix in which to understand and cognitively reprocess his problem.

As we reviewed some of Gabe's experiences over the previous decade, it appeared that his business had gone well, as had life in general.

His social life was focused. The patient preferred being single, with close friends and a few relatives, to an ongoing marriage and family commitment. In essence, nothing about his life jumped off the page, either for him or me, that could be used to develop into an example to build on as I sought to understand the ensuing disorder.

A Bomb Drops

As we went further back into what he remembered about his past, it became obvious that anxiety was a major part of his childhood. Both his mother and aunt had called him "nervous," he said, but since he had grown up in a war zone, he thought it was natural to have lasting anxieties and to be nervous. I jumped right in. "What war zone?"

Gabe told me that he had grown up "at a terrible time" in Great Britain during World War II. As a child barely out of diapers, he had experienced heavy bombings day after day in his hometown.

The patient clearly remembered being a child who heard bombs dropping on his town night after night. His ability to flash back to those bomb blasts from so long ago made me wonder whether Gabe would be a good subject for hypnosis to possibly enhance his memory.

Over the course of my career, I've become very comfortable using hypnosis. I've given many lectures and taught numerous educational programs on the use of medical hypnosis. In a few instances, with certain highly hypnotizable subjects, I have worked with age regression. Because of those experiences, I've learned how to differentiate between those who can truly age-regress and the simulators, who often think they're age regressing but are really just tapping memories or recollections from some other source of past events. True age regressors seem able to actually be in the moment when they go back in time. For example, while talking about their third birthday party, they will speak in a childlike voice.

This is not so when one simulates, describing a memory, or what has become memory from what they were told. Gabe did not appear to have many characteristics of those highly suggestible / hypnotizable people. Nevertheless, I did measure his hypnotizability, using an eye-roll test that I modified from Dr. Spiegel's five-minute test, where you have a patient roll his eyes up to the top of his head and slowly close his lids, taking deep breaths as he does this eye roll maneuver. This not only measures a patient's hypnotizability, it teaches him how to do this technique on his own as a way to relax.

As I suspected, Gabe was in the midrange, so he was not a candidate for age regression. As I measured his abilities, I made Gabe aware of every step I was taking and why I was doing it. He was clearly interested, and said that he wanted to go "back in time." I assured him that although he might be relaxed in the hypnotic experience, he would not be truly age regressed or "go back in time." But when he asked me, "Could I possibly remember something?" I answered, "Yes, you could."

Traveling Back in Time

So began our journey into this patient's memory, using a simple eye-roll and deep breathing technique. I asked questions about his life, decade by decade, but nothing remarkable came to light. I suggested that Gabe practice this relaxation technique on his own before our next visit to get more familiar with it.

On the third visit, using this hypnotic model, an amazing thing happened: Gabe clearly articulated his fears during the wartime bombings in his town. He revealed that, all those years ago, he had wished that he "would disappear" and "not be around" as the bomb blasts continued, and he recalled the sensations of terror and fear for his life. Gabe was very pleased by this revelation during his hypnotic recall. He did very well, and I figured he must have practiced a lot at home. In fact, he reported that he'd never practiced at all. That was a surprise. Being surprised and keeping a certain amount of flexibility when treating a person is good mental health care. It's good medical care as well.

I was pleased, but not very pleased. This memory had the potential to be a good source of the origins of primary symptoms of depersonalization, I explained, but it needed to be validated by outside confirmation. In my experience, when memories are evoked through hypnosis, they may not necessarily be reliable. I asked if there was anyone who could help him confirm this particular memory. No one came to mind, because no one else knew about Gabe's problems, except a few very close friends, and now me. He had been too embarrassed ever to mention those memories to anyone else.

I stressed that in order to go forward, I needed some corroboration of this memory as a method of validation. This is something I do routinely for any patient using hypnosis to enhance recall.

Gabe had an elderly aunt who had lived with his family at the time of the bombings and was the only person who might be able to help. After discussing this with me, he realized that he needed to ask her about his behaviors and thoughts while he was growing up. She confirmed the memory that all Gabe wanted to do, during the bombings and after, was to disappear. He reported that they all thought they were going to be killed at the time.

I was beginning to think, and now felt convinced, that Gabe was suffering from PTSD stemming from this early wartime trauma, of constant terror and fears that he and his family would be killed. The current data show that about 30 percent of PTSD sufferers have a dissociative reaction, and here was a case of PTSD occurring in an adult that was coupled to a dissociation disorder.

Learning How to Cope—on the Patient's Terms

With that confirmation, I was able to move quickly into the Learning phase of my LPA technique. In six visits, Gabe and I were able to cognitively challenge this learned processing of his very real fear of injury or death as a child. The aim was to focus on the effects of this learned experience and how it affected his bouts of dissociation. Over a period of time, he reported lessening of the "shrinking" experience, but it still plagued him. As we progressed, I also integrated the hypnotic model, which he had liked, into Gabe's treatment, and the split screen technique. I encouraged him to visualize the childhood trauma on his own large movie screen, putting a line down the middle of the screen and then visualizing the trauma on the left side only—just watching it, not going through it. We then linked this to visualizing pleasant experiences of his life on the right side of the screen, with the pleasant experiences overwhelming the trauma. He was really good at doing it. The symptoms of dissociation and depersonalization left him slowly, but they did leave.

Although I didn't immediately recognize Gabe's condition as rooted in PTSD, the combination of hypnosis and LPA techniques allowed him to unlock and release the traumatic memories that caused his dissociative disorder. I don't think any specific formula for treating dissociative disorders exists, since what's happening is very unclear and the *DSM* is less than adequate in its nomenclature. When the real neurochemistry, physiology, and imagery are scientifically elucidated—and this will happen—we'll move away from the pseudoscientific vocabulary of the *DSM* and understand more clearly exactly what we're treating. Until then, let's keep it simple, using cognitive, learning, and relearning techniques and relaxation/hypnotic approaches that appear to offer the best results for PTSD. Dissociative disorders need to be treated on an individual basis—by clinicians who have an open mind, and a broad base of experience and treatment strategies.

PTSD Case Study #3: Randi: Overcoming the Worst That Didn't Happen

When a single traumatic event triggers PTSD, some patients need an initial solution, and then want to explore the causes. Such was the case with Randi, whose PTSD stemmed from a dog bite.

She was in her forties, a divorced single mother with two teenagers. She lived in a middle-class Long Island suburb and worked as a human resources recruiter for an office a few blocks away from her home. She often walked to and from work. One wintry day, she passed a man walking a dog on a long leash. The dog suddenly jumped up and lunged at her, biting her on both arms. In her scramble to get away, Randi slipped on the icy sidewalk and shattered her left elbow.

The elbow injury landed her in the hospital, where she had to undergo surgery. She was also treated for the dog bites, which were relatively minor. The dog's owner was very distraught and cooperative. He provided all the paperwork to prove that his dog was in good health, and had all the required shots and an up-to-date license.

Rehab but not Recuperation

After the elbow surgery, Randi's orthopedic surgeon enrolled her in long, arduous program of physical therapy. This orthopedist was one those very attentive professionals who, after a successful surgical procedure, was open to discussing the patient's long-term recovery. He sensed Randi's lingering anxiety, noticing that as she talked about it over and over, she obsessed on what she had done wrong. Why hadn't she crossed the street? Why had she walked so close to the dog? "I could have hit my head on the pavement and died," she'd say over and over. She kept on reliving those traumatic moments, which she called "the fracture of my normal life." She couldn't sleep and was haunted by flashbacks.

Meanwhile, her physical recovery from a difficult surgery was actually going very well. And in follow-up visits and phone calls, it became clear to the orthopedist that Randi was traumatized emotionally — far more than many other patients with similar injuries. Three months past the incident, she was still in intense distress, and entirely focused on the emotional damage done. So the orthopedist referred her to me.

How to Forget

Randi had never been to a therapist in her life, and when she came into my office, she seemed a bit wary. Physically, she'd healed very well. I took a general history first: she had no apparent or overt history of emotional trauma in her past, was a college graduate, and liked her job. She seemed to have a lot friends and her social life had been active before the accident. In other words, she appeared to be a normal, well-functioning person.

Turning to talk of the accident, treatment and recovery, Randi's whole manner changed. Her face and voice grew tense, and I noticed her twisting her hands as she sat in the chair. As she told me what happened, she spent much more time on the before and after than the during. She was obsessed with thoughts of what she *should* have done—crossed the street to avoid the dog—and what *could* have happened. If she had hit her head any harder when she went down on the sidewalk, she insisted, she would have died.

Between Randi's obsession with her mistake in not crossing the street to avoid the dog, the endless loop of "*should haves, could haves, would haves*," the flashbacks, and the terrifying thought that her life could have ended, it was clear she was deep in the grip of PTSD. We spent some time defining PTSD, as well as the LPA technique we would use to treat her. Toward the end of the visit, Randi remarked that she'd never liked animals. I knew we'd be exploring this in future visits.

Learning from the Past

On our second visit, I hoped to reach a global philosophical understanding, based on Randi's history, of what might have precipitated such an extreme emotional response that she kept reliving it over and over. It was clear to me that the physical trauma of being attacked by the dog had caused Randi's emotional trauma. But her physical therapy and rehab were going well. She appeared to move her arm well and needed no painkillers. So why was she still terrified by the possibility that she could have died?

I tried to get Randi to talk about why she didn't like animals. She'd never had a dog or a cat growing up. Not surprisingly, her parents disliked pets. When Randi was a little girl, she was nipped on the hand by a cousin's puppy at a family occasion. It was a minor incident, barely a scratch, but her parents blew it up into a major scene, she told me.

So here was a pretty clear clue as to why Randi continued to beat herself up for not crossing the street as soon as she saw a dog coming her way. She had *learned* to dislike pets and had learned that even a minor nip was a horrible event — so horrible that it helped to create her PTSD response. But Randi wasn't here to dig up the roots of her reasons for disliking dogs. If she wanted to pursue this issue further, she could work it out with a CBT or LPA program, or even a traditional talk therapist. My job was treating her PTSD and freeing her from the emotional distress that was taking over her life.

We continued to the Action phase of LPA. Using PTSD as the main problem, I began by teaching her the self-hypnosis/relaxation technique called reciprocal inhibition, pioneered by Dr. Joseph Wolpe over a half a century ago. This relaxation technique is usually incompatible with anxiety, and as Randi practiced, I could see her begin to relax, with her physical tension lessening. She was actually calming her mind. It took her about thirty minutes to master the basics.

Randi's Split Screen

Then I added the split-screen visualization technique. Over a period of several visits, we developed a hierarchy of events, going from non-stressful to very stressful, that Randi projected onto the left half of the screen. Unlike the flashbacks that plagued her, she was *seeing* these events, not *experiencing* them. That's the key: the witness is also the "movie director," and completely in control of what she's seeing.

We started with visualizations of Randi leaving her office, walking down a quiet street in her familiar suburban neighborhood, looking forward to seeing her children, and having a nice dinner. This led to the man walking the dog, and then to the dog lunging toward her. Seen instead of experienced, controlled, and watched at her own pace, her anxiety was kept to a minimum. And she agreed to practice this at home, at least three times a day, until these images were so familiar—seen from a distance—that she felt safe. And on the right side of her movie screen, Randi projected pleasant, happier scenes, anything she wanted. She had plenty.

By linking the projected visualizations of the traumatic event with pleasant visualized experiences, the images on the right side begin to overcome those on the left. In time, traumatic events are linked to perceived pleasure. Soon, most of Randi's PTSD was resolved: while she still remembered the event, she was free of the flashbacks and nightmares, and her obsessive *could-haves, would-haves, should-haves* were greatly diminished. She had learned to relax, and basically felt much better. She even made it a point to thank her orthopedist for the referral. But unlike many other patients, she wanted to keep talking. She wanted to work out why she disliked dogs and cats, and how this might have affected her emotional response. She also wanted to work on ways to improve her social life and get into a good relationship. None of this had come out in the original history when she was too upset to think about other life issues. But free of anxiety, she felt brave enough to explore this.

So we spent another three months using LPA to explore her dislike of pets and why her relationships weren't moving forward. It turned out that Randi had an obsessive personality, both at work and at home. She was extremely concerned with her children's performance in school, and very critical of the men she met. She was also a fast learner. Continuing the talk therapy using my LPA technique worked well.

A year later, when she came in for a follow-up, she was doing wonderfully. She had come to grips with her PTSD, worked on some other issues, and was feeling good. She had actually met a man when he was out walking his Golden Retriever, she said, and it was a lovely dog. They'd struck up a conversation. And now, she was looking forward to getting to know them both.

CHAPTER 13

Can't Sleep? Try These Three Strategies

In 2016, the American College of Physicians, which represents the largest number of primary care doctors in the United States, recommended Cognitive Behavioral Therapy as first-line treatment for chronic insomnia.

I couldn't agree more that it should be part of first-line treatment for insomnia. Furthermore, I believe that using CBT for sleeping problems rather than a "pill" is preferable. However, CBT does require several office visits and could go on for many months with diaries kept and sleep pattern analyses, including relearning methods of falling asleep and staying asleep. The other part of first-line treatments should be guided imagery techniques, which also eliminate the use of pills, and are effective, quicker, and more economical.

The Action phase of my own version of CBT—LPA—can help people fall asleep in one or two visits using relaxation and guided imagery. Those strategies can be used before shifting to a more difficult and lengthy process of CBT, which not only examines sleeping patterns over a period of many weeks and sometimes months, but often includes examining life stressors and life tensions that either keep people awake or prevent them from a restful sleep.

Before starting this very short-term method of treating insomnia, however, it's important to take a history of physical or mental problems, and assessing whether the relaxation and guided imagery will be helpful. For example, certain physical, mental, and chronic pain problems might not be amenable to CBT or relaxation and guided imagery. In those cases, other methods need to be explored by the proper clinician treating those problems.

Here are three specific strategies for treating insomnia:

1. Visualize twenty heavily carpeted stairs, and make them your favorite color while trying to fall asleep. Imagine yourself slowly walking down these stairs and letting yourself fall into a restful sleep by the time you reach the bottom step. This process, and those below, can be used multiple times.

2. Allow yourself to imagine a great big movie screen, and on that screen project some of the favorite experiences or things you plan to do in the future. Often, this technique allows a person to fall into a restful sleep.

3. Imagine a large, red balloon attached to a wicker gondola, and put all of your worries and anxieties into that gondola. Allow the red balloon to float into a very blue, blue sky, and watch the red balloon get smaller and smaller into that blue sky until you find yourself drifting off into a restful sleep.

As a second tier, we can always do the longer CBT method, which I also believe is preferable to taking medication if the shorter, more efficient method is not working. In other words, like psychotherapy, the shortest, most efficient methods should go first, just as is the case in other medical specialties.

CHAPTER 14

Conclusion: Treating with Compassion

It's hard to imagine a more diverse group of personalities than the composite of examples you've met in this book. Each example had a very specific problem that made their lives more stressful and difficult than they wanted. Something stood in the way of their happiness, and they wanted help solving it. By sitting down together for a short time and taking a focused look at the problem at hand, challenging the thinking that caused it to take root, and learning new behaviors and strategies, each one of them found relief.

These examples are just a few of the many people I've seen in my years of practice. It is deeply satisfying to help people work through a problem they never thought they would be able to solve. Of course, there are some situations where LPA doesn't produce good results — and I've never had a problem referring to other psychiatrists, psychologists, or other therapists for a different type of therapy.

I developed my LPA method after many years of assessing what people wanted when seeking talk therapy in the mental health field, how their minds processed information, and what would help give them a new outlook and coping skills to handle their problems as quickly and effectively as possible.

Much in the field of mental functioning remains a mystery when it comes to understanding how our brains work and how our intellect, emotions, and memory interact as we try to solve mental problems.

To make matters worse, there are a dizzying number of options for those seeking help. When you start adding up all the different approaches, there seem to be hundreds or even thousands of psychotherapies practiced, some by licensed or certified professionals and others who simply call themselves therapists of one kind or another.

Unfortunately, many of these treatment approaches fail to resolve the problems that led patients to seek help in the first place. Despite the mind's mysteries, we do know that learning, relearning, and learning anew is not only possible, but can be well-documented. As a method of therapy, learning new ideas, concepts, and behaviors can be codified, just as the information we learn in school can be codified. Learning and relearning even coordinates well with new concepts of evidence-based medicine. I believe that, along with evidence, great medical clinicians are gifted with knowledge and experience when caring for the sick and troubled.

When someone seeks mental health help to fix a specific problem, I use the knowledge and experience of focused learning theory methods, just as the orthopedic surgeon focuses on what bone is broken or the ophthalmologist focuses on the eye that has the problem. This seems like common sense, yet common sense is not always at the core of mental health care, as it is with other branches of medicine. But if there is a problem with a specific part of the mental "house," we don't have to burn down the house, or the whole town, to fix it. If the roof is leaking, let's look at the roof.

As you've seen from the case studies of people suffering from various phobias, post-traumatic stress disorder, anxiety and other disorders, my LPA method can work for people struggling with a wide variety of issues.

I hope this book has given you a better understanding of focused short-term psychotherapy as a viable mental health care option for many problems that often get bogged down in much longer treatments.

Long-term therapeutic approaches often fail to address the specific problem at hand, focusing instead on feelings and emotional history. Though clearly these play a role, long-term therapies rarely circumscribe the problem in a thoughtful manner, and offer new perspectives and practical steps to address the problem and make lasting changes to thought patterns and behaviors.

There are large number of mental health approaches and psychotherapies available to those seeking help, some tried and true, some more anecdotal, and some that go on indefinitely. Getting familiar with these options allows you to be a better consumer and to make intelligent choices when seeking care in a very complicated and diverse field.

It has always been my belief that short-term therapies work best as a first approach to care before moving into open-ended treatment approaches if more exploration is needed. To revisit the mental "house," once your roof has stopped leaking, you may want to look at the structural problems that caused it to leak. But starting from the foundation and wandering through every room while the roof continues to leak makes no sense. Nor does using psychopharmacology in certain cases as an umbrella, which might cover the symptoms, but does nothing to fix the actual leak, and will only keep working as long as you keep taking those medications.

It is important for a person seeking help to ask a psychiatrist, psychologist, psychiatric social worker, or psychiatric nurse practitioner whether they begin care with a view to short-term problem resolution as the first line of therapy. The consumer might also question whether the therapy they offer is open-ended or has a particular time frame. Does it seem like a practical, common sense approach? Are the mental health practitioner's questions directed at how to gain different perspectives on past experiences, change thought processes and behaviors in order to move forward with your life and make it better, or are most of the questions about the deep past and who is to blame? Does this practitioner seem to work from the assumption that the answer to most mental problems is finding the right medication?

The focus of this book is on short-term talk therapy. But clearly, many medication-based approaches for specific mental disorders are effective, and the pharmaceutical breakthroughs of the '50s and '60s and subsequent modifications have alleviated a great deal of pain and suffering in many with severe mental illnesses and biochemical imbalances. But often in clinical practice today, medications are prescribed for myriad disorders—including phobias, PTSD, and certain anxiety issues as reported in this book, as well as for personality disorders— which I will discuss in more detail in my next book. Non-medicinal approaches often times not only work better, they are longer-lasting. The rule of thumb seems to be "When in doubt, try a pill." If it doesn't work, try a *different* pill, or a combination of pills. Over time, more and more prescription medicines may be added to the "cocktail" with minimal results, and sometimes with harmful side effects.

It's also worth noting that symptoms can easily be misdiagnosed and consequently mistreated. The hallucinations of somebody undergoing a schizophrenic episode are different from a person's thoughts just as flashbacks experienced by someone whose PTSD has been triggered by a specific trauma are different from memories. An inexperienced clinician may hear a person describe "hallucinations" which are really thoughts and jump to conclusions, medicating for an underlying condition the patient does not actually have. If you do have a condition that requires medication, of course you should take it. But please be assured that many mental health problems can be resolved by Learning, Philosophizing, and Action or other variants of CBT.

I hope you have found this book useful for gaining a deeper understanding of how the mind works, how we learn and relearn, and the many approaches to solving the problems that stand in the way of our happiness. Remember, *you* are the consumer when it comes to mental health resources. The choice is always yours, and it's my hope that you'll seek out and choose the method of treatment that helps you to find freedom fast.

Books

Beck, Aaron T., Arthur Freeman, Denise D. Davis, and Associates. *Cognitive Therapy of Personality Disorders.* New York: The Guilford Press, 1990.

Bourne, Edmund J. *The Anxiety & Phobia Workbook.* 4th ed. Oakland, Calif.: New Harbinger Publications, 2005.

Burns, David D. *Feeling Good: The New Mood Therapy.* New York: William Morrow & Co., 1980.

Crasilneck, Harold B. and James A. Hall. Clinical Hypnosis: Principles and Applications. New York: Grune & Stratton, 1975.

Dobson, Keith S., ed. *Handbook of Cognitive-Behavioral Therapies.* 2d ed. New York: The Guilford Press, 2001.

Fenichel, Otto. *The Psychoanalytic Theory of Neurosis.* New York: W.W. Norton & Co. Inc., 1996.

Frankel, Fred H. Hypnosis: Trance as a Coping Mechanism. New York: Plenum Medical Book Co., 1976.

Greenson, Ralph R. *The Technique and Practice of Psychoanalysis.* New York: International Universities Press, 1972.

Hale, Nathan G., Jr. *Freud and The Americans: The Beginnings of Psychoanalysis in the United States, 1876-1917.* Vol. 1. London: Oxford University Press, 1971.

———, *Freud and The Americans: The Beginnings of Psychoanalysis in the United States, 1917-1985.* Vol. 2. London: Oxford University Press, 1995.

Kroger, William S. *Clinical and Experimental Hypnosis in Medicine, Dentistry, and Psychology.* Philadelphia: J.B. Lippincott & Co., 1963.

Kroger, William S. *Clinical and Experimental Hypnosis in Medicine, Dentistry, and Psychology.* Philadelphia: Lippincott Williams & Wilkins, a Wolters Kluwer business, 2008.

Kroger, William S. and William D. Fezler. *Hypnosis and Behavior Modification: Imagery Conditioning.* Philadelphia: J.B. Lippincott & Co., 1976.

Lieberman, Jeffrey A. *Shrinks: The Untold Story of Psychiatry.* 1st ed. Boston: Little, Brown and Company, 2015.

Masters, David C. and John C. Rimm. *Behavior Therapy: Techniques and Empirical Findings.* New York and London: Academic Press, 1974.

Messer, Stanley B. and C. Seth Warren. *Models of Brief Psychodynamic Therapy: A Comparative Approach.* New York: The Guilford Press, 1995.

Sadock, Benjamin James, Virginia Alcott Sadock and Pedro Ruiz. *Kaplan and Sadock's Synopsis of Psychiatry.* 11th ed. Philadelphia: Lippincott Williams & Wilkins, 2015.

Shiraldi, Glenn R. *The Post-Traumatic Stress Disorder Sourcebook.* 1st ed. New York: McGraw-Hill Education, 2016.

Sifneos, Peter E. *Short-Term Psychotherapy and Emotional Crisis.* 4th printing. Cambridge, Mass.: Harvard University Press, 1978.

Southwick, Steven M. and Dennis S. Charney. *Resilience: The Science of Mastering Life's Challenges.* 11th printing. Cambridge, England: Cambridge University Press/Sheridan Books, 2016.

Spiegel, Herbert and David Spiegel. *Trance and Treatment.* 2d ed. Washington, D.C.: American Psychiatric Association Publishing, 2004.

Sudak, Donna M. *Cognitive Behavioral Therapy for Clinicians.* Philadelphia: Lippincott Williams & Wilkins, 2006.

Wolberg, Lewis R. *Short-Term Psychotherapy*. New York: Grune & Stratton, 1965.

———, *The Technique of Psychotherapy*. vol. 1 & 2, 2d ed. New York: Grune & Stratton, 1967.

Wolpe, Joseph. *The Practice of Behavioral Therapy*. 2d ed. Oxford: Pergamon Press Inc., 1970.

Other References

Araujo, D.M. "Anxiety during pregnancy, prematurity, and low birth weight: a systematic literature review." Cadernos de Saude Publica. 2007 Apr;23(4):747-56.

Diagnostic and Statistical Manual of Mental Disorders: DSM-5. Arlington, Va.: American Psychiatric Association, 2013.

Diagnostic and Statistical Manual of Mental Disorders: DSM-IV. Washington, D.C.: American Psychiatric Association, 1994.

Diagnostic and Statistical Manual of Mental Disorders: DSM-III. Washington, D.C.: American Psychiatric Association, 1980.

Diagnostic and Statistical Manual of Mental Disorders: DSM-II. Washington, D.C.: American Psychiatric Association, 1968.

About the Author

Robert T. London, MD, is a well-known psychiatrist, educator, and writer known for his ability to translate complex medical concepts into accessible information and practical strategies for general audiences and mental health professionals alike. Through his appearances on television, radio, in print, and online, he aims to push the door to the psychiatrist's and therapist's office wide open so people can talk freely about their mental health concerns.

Dr. London delivers a message of hope and optimism to the thousands of people he's treated, and passionately believes that many people with mental health conditions can achieve significant improvement or total relief. What's more, it doesn't have to take years in therapy.

Dr. London has been a practicing physician/psychiatrist for four decades. For 20 years, he developed and ran the short-term psychotherapy unit at the NYU Langone Medical Center, where he specialized and developed numerous short-term cognitive therapy techniques. He also offers his expertise as a consulting psychiatrist.

In the 1970s, Dr. London was host of his own consumer-oriented health care radio program, which was syndicated nationally. In the 1980s, he created "Evening with the Doctors," a three-hour town hall style meeting for nonmedical audiences—the forerunner to today's TV show "The Doctors." Over the years, he has appeared on "Good Morning America," "Live at Five," "Eyewitness News," "Good Day New York," the Cable News Network, and has been quoted extensively in *The New York Times, the New York Daily News, the New York Post, Newsday, Businessweek, the Los Angeles Times*, among other news outlets.

He has penned well over a hundred articles and columns, and has appeared in many publications, "including the *New England Journal of Medicine, JAMA, Glamour,* and *On the Avenue,* the late NYC cultural magazine for which he wrote a regular medical column during the 1980s. Throughout the '80s, he also was medical editor for Long Island's *Boulevard* magazine and wrote its popular "To Your Health" column.

Dr. London is best known as the long-time author of "The Psychiatrist's Toolbox," a nationally distributed monthly column in *Clinical Psychiatry News,* which is now available online and is sold around the globe by the Frontline Medical News wire service. He continues to be an editorial contributor to *Clinical Psychiatry News.*

ENDORSEMENTS

"Now you can find freedom fast like never before. Internationally renowned psychiatrist Dr. Robert London shares his unique and innovative approach to treating common emotional problems quickly and thoroughly. With empathy and compassion, Dr. London guides readers through a series of steps to get to the root of the problem fast and provide lasting relief. This book is a must-read for those facing anxiety disorders, phobias, or post-traumatic stress syndrome who want to find freedom fast. Dr. London's step-by-step approach, using real life examples, will show you how to overcome your problem in no time."
—Elishka Caneva, MD, Psychiatrist, Clinical Director, Partial Hospital Program, St. Vincent's Hospital, Harrison, NY

"Dr. London presents a most refreshing approach to psychotherapy and adds a very personal and engaging perspective along the way. The vivid clinical vignettes present a highly compelling narrative portrayal of the straightforward yet elegant nature of each individual's journey."
—Richard A. Oberfield, MD, Clinical Professor of Psychiatry, NYU School of Medicine

"Dr. London is a voice of reason, who acts as a beacon in the quagmire of ineffective talk therapy. His LPA approach moves straight to the presenting problem by teaching individuals how to apply a simple technique that can be utilized for a lifetime. Anyone who implements the wisdom provided in this book is sure to witness their life grow exponentially for the better."
—Maria Leventis-DiStefano, Psychiatric Mental Health Nurse Practitioner

"As a psycho-dynamically oriented therapist myself, I was intrigued to learn new techniques for treating acute anxiety and specific traumas, and this book delivers. Dr. London's heart and soul shine through on every page, which makes me believe his empathy and compassion are just as healing to his patients as the techniques he so skillfully illustrates. Highly recommended for those still in training, as well as established professionals in the field. His writing is concise, approachable, warm, and illuminating."
—**Michelle C. Crimins, PhD, Licensed Psychologist**

"Dr. London's new book, *Find Freedom Fast,* is a must-read for both patients and clinicians. Written in his clear, straightforward style, he provides practical advice and outlines a clear path and specific steps to effectively feel better without long-term, open-ended treatment. Clinicians will benefit from his insights from a long-term career benefiting hundreds of patients and having been a part of their own improved mental health and life adjustment. He lays out the path but the patient finds their own specific solutions that best suits them! Wise advice."
—**Nicole Breck, Mental Health Therapist; Licensed Clinical Social Worker [LCSW]**

INDEX

Made in the USA
Middletown, DE
16 February 2019